THE NATION'S
FAVOURITE POEMS
OF REMEMBRANCE

— e —

FOREWORD BY
MICHAEL ROSEN

BBC
BOOKS

Published by
BBC Books,
BBC Worldwide Limited,
Woodlands,
80 Wood Lane,
London
W12 0TT

First published 2003
Edited and compiled by Alex Warwick
Compilation © BBC Worldwide 2003
Poems © individual copyright holders

ISBN: 0 563 48769 0

Set in Stempel Garamond by Keystroke,
Jacaranda Lodge, Wolverhampton.
Printed and bound in Great Britain by Martins the Printers Ltd,
Berwick-upon-Tweed.
Cover printed by Belmont Press, Northampton.

The Poetry Society has been promoting poets and poetry
in Britain since 1909. A membership organisation open to all,
it publishes Britain's leading poetry magazine, *Poetry Review*,
runs the National Poetry Competition, has a lively education
programme and offers advice and information on reading
and writing poetry. For further information
telephone 020 7420 9880 or
email info@poetrysoc.com
www.poetrysoc.com

THE POETRY SOCIETY

CONTENTS

— e —

– Contents –

'Most near, most dear, most loved and most far...'

'The greatest griefs shall find
themselves inside the smallest cage'

'But if the while I think on thee, dear friend'

– Contents –

7

– Contents –

– Contents –

FOREWORD

BY MICHAEL ROSEN

— e —

You can't escape from memory. You can't even escape from the things that you think you've forgotten. Our memories scurry about out of sight, in a warren, sometimes popping up to take a look at us, to surprise us; one moment delighting us, the next – offering us a warning that something we might not like is getting close; and then as we take notice, they often pop back, out of sight, scurrying about in the warren again.

And yet, they're more mysterious than that. Memories might seem to be like animals with lives of their own, appearing at times to control us, or even to make us their prisoners. The truth is, it was us who put them there in the first place. We made them. But here you are, laughing like your mother, whistling like your friend from school, running towards a love that will harm you even as you were once harmed. So, can it be that we make our own memories even as our memories are making us?

I spend a lot of time in my warren. There are real pleasures in there, but sadnesses too. For some people that's quite enough to be dealing with: spending time with a few memories and then trying to get on. I'm someone who not only spends time in there but also someone who asks himself over and over again, what shall I do with all this? For years, this was an exciting game of hide and seek: what about those washing up fights my brother and I had? What about that time my friend and I walked out of Wales into England with our trousers down? Write them down, share them, enjoy them.

Then, in 1999, my dear son Eddie, who I had written about as a hilarious and rumbustious toddler, died. He was nearly 19. From under the frightening wave of feelings, I was sure that I wouldn't and couldn't write about what had happened. And so it was for about a year and a half. Then, slowly out of the wave, I was able to pull out a few strings of words, riffs and sequences that seemed to say back to me how I was feeling. In that very act, there was some kind of relief from what had seemed like an endless pressure. To write what I felt and to read

11

what I had written seemed to allow something out. It also joined me to a place where I wasn't alone. I could now stop myself from thinking that I was the only person in the whole world who had ever lost a son, a child, a much-loved person. It happens.

This fine book seems to me about how we can discover that even at our most lonely moment, we are not alone. If you've picked it up at a moment of grief or despair, I think you'll find strings, riffs and sequences that you will want to grab and remember. After all, there is hundreds of years' worth of grieving, thinking and writing here. And who knows, in the shortfall between the feelings you have when you read and the feelings you have doing your own remembering, you may want to pull out some strings, riffs and sequences of your own. For others, stopping here to wonder what news poets bring from the other side of sadness, this book has many moments and many meanings on a matter that has every-thing to do with how we live. I'm re-reading it.

'Our two soules . . .'

from 'A Valediction: Forbidding Mourning'

THOMAS HARDY 1840–1928

THE VOICE

Woman much missed, how you call to me, call to me,
Saying that now you are not as you were
When you had changed from the one who was all to me,
But as at first, when our day was fair.

Can it be you that I hear? Let me view you, then,
Standing as when I drew near to the town
Where you would wait for me: yes, as I knew you then,
Even to the original air-blue gown!

Or is it only the breeze, in its listlessness
Travelling across the wet mead to me here,
You being ever dissolved to wan wistlessness,
Heard no more again far or near?

   Thus I; faltering forward,
   Leaves around me falling,
Wind oozing thin through the thorn from norward,
   And the woman calling.

JOHN MILTON 1608–74

'METHOUGHT I SAW MY LATE ESPOUSÈD SAINT'

Methought I saw my late espousèd saint
Brought to me like Alcestis from the grave,
Whom Jove's great son to her glad husband gave,
Rescued from death by force, though pale and faint.
Mine, as whom washed from spot of child-bed taint
Purification in the old Law did save,
And such, as yet once more I trust to have
Full sight of her in heaven without restraint,
Came vested all in white, pure as her mind.
Her face was veiled; yet to my fancied sight
Love, sweetness, goodness in her person shined
So clear as in no face with more delight.
But O, as to embrace me she inclined,
I waked, she fled, and day brought back my night.

KATHERINE, LADY DYER ?–1654

EPITAPH ON SIR WILLIAM DYER

My dearest dust could not thy hasty day
Afford thy drowzy patience leave to stay
One hower longer; so that we might either
      Sate up, or gone to bedd together?
But since thy finisht labor hath possest
      Thy weary limbs with early rest,
Enjoy it sweetly; and thy widdowe bride
Shall soone repose her by thy slumbring side;
Whose business, now is only to prepare
      My nightly dress, and call to prayre:
Mine eyes wax heavy and the day growes old
      The dew falls thick, my bloud growes cold;
Draw, draw the closed curtaynes and make roome:
My deare, my dearest dust; I come, I come.

HENRY KING 1592–1669

from THE EXEQUY. TO HIS MATCHLESS
NEVER TO BE FORGOTTEN FRIEND

Sleep on my *Love* in thy cold bed
Never to be disquieted!
My last good night! Thou wilt not wake
Till I thy fate shall overtake:
Till age, or grief, or sickness must
Marry my body to that dust
It so much loves; and fill the room
My heart keeps empty in thy Tomb.
Stay for me there; I will not faile
To meet thee in that hollow Vale.
And think not much of my delay;
I am already on the way,
And follow thee with all the speed
Desire can make, or sorrows breed.
Each minute is a short degree,
And ev'ry houre a step towards thee.
At night when I betake to rest,
Next morn I rise neerer my West
Of life, almost by eight houres saile,
That when sleep breath'd his drowsie gale.

Thus from the Sun my Bottom stears,
And my dayes Compass downward bears:
Nor labour I to stemme the tide
Through which to *Thee* I swiftly glide.

Tis true, with shame and grief I yield,
Thou like the *Vann* first took'st the field,
And gotten hast the victory
In thus adventuring to dy
Before me, whose more years might crave
A just precedence in the grave.
But heark! My pulse like a soft Drum

18

Beats my approach, tells *Thee* I come;
And slow howere my marches be,
I shall at last sit down by *Thee*.

   The thought of this bids me go on,
And wait my dissolution
With hope and comfort. *Dear* (forgive
The crime) I am content to live
Divided, with but half a heart,
Till we shall meet and never part.

JOHN DONNE 1572–1631

A VALEDICTION: FORBIDDING MOURNING

As virtuous men passe mildly'away,
   And whisper to their soules, to goe,
Whilst some of their sad friends doe say,
   The breath goes now, and some say, no:

So let us melt, and make no noise,
   No teare-floods, nor sigh-tempests move,
'Twere prophanation of our joyes
   To tell the layetie our love.

Moving of th'earth brings harmes and feares,
   Men reckon what it did and meant,
But trepidation of the spheares,
   Though greater farre, is innocent.

Dull sublunary lovers love
   (Whose soule is sense) cannot admit
Absence, because it doth remove
   Those things which elemented it.

But we by'a love, so much refin'd,
   That our selves know not what it is,
Inter-assured of the mind,
   Care lesse, eyes, lips, and hands to misse.

Our two soules therefore, which are one,
   Though I must goe, endure not yet
A breach, but an expansion,
   Like gold to ayery thinnesse beate.

If they be two, they are two so
   As stiffe twin compasses are two,
Thy soule the fixt foot, makes no show
   To move, but doth, if the'other doe.

And though it in the center sit,
   Yet when the other far doth rome,
It leanes, and hearkens after it,
   And growes erect, as it comes home.

Such wilt thou be to mee, who must
   Like th'other foot, obliquely runne;
Thy firmnes makes my circle just,
   And makes me end, where I begunne.

PHILIP LARKIN 1922–85

AN ARUNDEL TOMB

Side by side, their faces blurred,
The earl and countess lie in stone,
Their proper habits vaguely shown
As jointed armour, stiffened pleat,
And that faint hint of the absurd –
The little dogs under their feet.

Such plainness of the pre-baroque
Hardly involves the eye, until
It meets his left-hand gauntlet, still
Clasped empty in the other; and
One sees, with a sharp tender shock
His hand withdrawn, holding her hand.

They would not think to lie so long.
Such faithfulness in effigy
Was just a detail friends would see:
A sculptor's sweet commissioned grace
Thrown off in helping to prolong
The Latin names around the base.

They would not guess how early in
Their supine stationary voyage
The air would change to soundless damage,
Turn the old tenantry away;
How soon succeeding eyes begin
To look, not read. Rigidly they

Persisted, linked, through lengths and breadths
Of time. Snow fell, undated. Light
Each summer thronged the glass. A bright
Litter of birdcalls strewed the same
Bone-riddled ground. And up the paths
The endless altered people came,

Washing at their identity.
Now, helpless in the hollow of
An unarmorial age, a trough
Of smoke in slow suspended skeins
Above their scrap of history,
Only an attitude remains:

Time has transfigured them into
Untruth. The stone fidelity
They hardly meant has come to be
Their final blazon, and to prove
Our almost-instinct almost true:
What will survive of us is love.

CHARLOTTE MEW 1869–1928

À QUOI BON DIRE

Seventeen years ago you said
    Something that sounded like Good-bye;
    And everybody thinks that you are dead,
        But I.

    So I, as I grow stiff and cold
To this and that say Good-bye too;
    And everybody sees that I am old
        But you.

    And one fine morning in a sunny lane
Some boy and girl will meet and kiss and swear
    That nobody can love their way again
        While over there
You will have smiled, I shall have tossed your hair.

LOUIS MACNEICE 1907–63

from AUTUMN JOURNAL

September has come and I wake
    And I think with joy how whatever, now or in future, the system
Nothing whatever can take
    The people away, there will always be people
For friends or for lovers though perhaps
    The conditions of love will be changed and its vices diminished
And affection not lapse
    To narrow possessiveness, jealousy founded on vanity.
September has come, it is *hers*
    Whose vitality leaps in the autumn,
Whose nature prefers
    Trees without leaves and a fire in the fire-place;
So I give her this month and the next
    Though the whole of my year should be hers who has rendered already
So many of its days intolerable or perplexed
    But so many more so happy;
Who has left a scent on my life and left my walls
    Dancing over and over with her shadow,
Whose hair is twined in all my waterfalls
    And all of London littered with remembered kisses.
So I am glad
    That life contains her with her moods and moments
More shifting and more transient than I had
    Yet thought of as being integral to beauty;
Whose mind is like the wind on a sea of wheat,
    Whose eyes are candour,
And assurance in her feet
    Like a homing pigeon never by doubt diverted.
To whom I send my thanks
    That the air has become shot silk, the streets are music,
And that the ranks
    Of men are ranks of men, no more of cyphers.
So that if now alone
    I must pursue this life, it will not be only

A drag from numbered stone to numbered stone
  But a ladder of angels, river turning tidal.
Off-hand, at times hysterical, abrupt,
  You are one I always shall remember,
Whom cant can never corrupt
  Nor argument disinherit.
Frivolous, always in a hurry, forgetting the address,
  Frowning too often, taking enormous notice
Of hats and backchat – how could I assess
  The thing that makes you different?
You whom I remember glad or tired,
  Smiling in drink or scintillating anger,
Inopportunely desired
  On boats, on trains, on roads when walking.
Sometimes untidy, often elegant,
  So easily hurt, so readily responsive,
To whom a trifle could be an irritant
  Or could be balm and manna.
Whose words would tumble over each other and pelt
  From pure excitement,
Whose fingers curl and melt
  When you were friendly.
I shall remember you in bed with bright
  Eyes or in a café stirring coffee
Abstractedly and on your plate the white
  Smoking stub your lips had touched with crimson.
And I shall remember how your words could hurt
  Because they were so honest
And even your lies were able to assert
  Integrity of purpose.
And it is on the strength of knowing you
  I reckon generous feeling more important
Than the mere deliberating what to do
  When neither the pros nor cons affect the pulses.

And though I have suffered from your special strength
  Who never flatter for points nor fake responses
I should be proud if I could evolve at length
  An equal thrust and pattern.

TED HUGHES 1930–98

THE STONE

Has not yet been cut.
It is too heavy already
For consideration. Its edges
Are so super-real, already,
And at this distance,
They cut real cuts in the unreal
Stuff of just thinking. So I leave it.
Somewhere it is.
Soon it will come.
I shall not carry it. With horrible life
It will transport its face, with sure strength,
To sit over mine, wherever I look,
Instead of hers.
It will even have across its brow
Her name.

Somewhere it is coming to the end
Of its million million years –
Which have worn her out.
It is coming to the beginning
Of her million million million years
Which will wear out it.

Because she will never move now
Till it is worn out.
She will not move now
Till everything is worn out.

'It isn't in important situations that I miss you'

from 'Attempts at the Rational Approach'

LAURENCE BINYON 1869–1943

WINTER SUNRISE

It is early morning within this room: without,
Dark and damp: without and within, stillness
Waiting for day: not a sound but a listening air.

Yellow jasmine, delicate on stiff branches
Stands in a Tuscan pot to delight the eye
In spare December's patient nakedness.

Suddenly, softly, as if at a breath breathed
On the pale wall, a magical apparition,
The shadow of the jasmine, branch and blossom!

It was not there, it is there, in a perfect image;
And all is changed. It is like a memory lost
Returning without a reason into the mind;

And it seems to me that the beauty of the shadow
Is more beautiful than the flower; a strange beauty,
Pencilled and silently deepening to distinctness.

As a memory stealing out of the mind's slumber,
A memory floating up from a dark water,
Can be more beautiful than the thing remembered.

ALFRED, LORD TENNYSON 1809–92

from 'IN MEMORIAM' A. H. H.

XIV

If one should bring me this report,
   That thou hadst touch'd the land to-day,
   And I went down unto the quay,
And found thee lying in the port;

And standing, muffled round with woe,
   Should see thy passengers in rank
   Come stepping lightly down the plank,
And beckoning unto those they know;

And if along with these should come
   The man I held as half-divine;
   Should strike a sudden hand in mine,
And ask a thousand things of home;

And I should tell him all my pain,
   And how my life had droop'd of late,
   And he should sorrow o'er my state
And marvel what possess'd my brain;

And I perceived no touch of change,
   No hint of death in all his frame,
   But found him all in all the same,
I should not feel it to be strange.

W.S. GRAHAM 1918–86

LINES ON ROGER HILTON'S WATCH

Which I was given because
I loved him and we had
Terrible times together.

O tarnished ticking time
Piece with your bent hand,
You must be used to being
Looked at suddenly
In the middle of the night
When he switched the light on
Beside his bed. I hope
You told him the best time
When he lifted you up
To meet the Hilton gaze.

I lift you up from the mantel
Piece here in my house
Wearing your verdigris.
At least I keep you wound
And put my ear to you
To hear Botallack tick.

You realise your master
Has relinquished you
And gone to lie under
The ground at St Just.

Tell me the time. The time
Is Botallack o'clock.
This is the dead of night.

He switches the light on
To find a cigarette
And pours himself a Teachers.
He picks me up and holds me
Near his lonely face
To see my hands. He thinks
He is not being watched.

The images of his dream
Are still about his face
As he spits and tries not
To remember where he was.

I am only a watch
And pray time hastes away.
I think I am running down.

Watch, it is time I wound
You up again. I am
Very much not your dear
Last master but we had
Terrible times together.

WALT WHITMAN 1819–92

from 'WHEN LILACS LAST IN THE DOORYARD BLOOM'D'

When lilacs last in the dooryard bloom'd,
And the great star early droop'd in the western sky in the night,
I mourn'd, and yet shall mourn with ever-returning spring.

Ever-returning spring, trinity sure to me you bring,
Lilac blooming perennial and drooping star in the west,
And thought of him I love.

THOMAS HARDY 1840–1928

AT CASTLE BOTEREL

As I drive to the junction of lane and highway,
    And the drizzle bedrenches the waggonette,
I look behind at the fading byway,
    And see on its slope, now glistening wet,
        Distinctly yet

Myself and a girlish form benighted
    In dry March weather. We climb the road
Beside a chaise. We had just alighted
    To ease the sturdy pony's load
        When he sighed and slowed.

What we did as we climbed, and what we talked of
    Matters not much, nor to what it led, –
Something that life will not be balked of
    Without rude reason till hope is dead,
        And feeling fled.

It filled but a minute. But was there ever
    A time of such quality, since or before,
In that hill's story? To one mind never,
    Though it has been climbed, foot-swift, foot-sore,
        By thousands more.

Primaeval rocks form the road's steep border,
    And much have they faced there, first and last,
Of the transitory in Earth's long order;
    But what they record in colour and cast
        Is – that we two passed.

And to me, though Time's unflinching rigour,
    In mindless rote, has ruled from sight
The substance now, one phantom figure
    Remains on the slope, as when that night
        Saw us alight.

I look and see it there, shrinking, shrinking,
    I look back at it amid the rain
For the very last time; for my sand is sinking,
    And I shall traverse old love's domain
        Never again.

WILLIAM ALLINGHAM 1824–89

'EVERYTHING PASSES AND VANISHES'

Everything passes and vanishes;
Everything leaves its trace;
And often you see in a footstep
What you could not see in a face.

D.H. LAWRENCE 1885–1930

SORROW

Why does the thin grey strand
Floating up from the forgotten
Cigarette between my fingers,
Why does it trouble me?

Ah, you will understand;
When I carried my mother downstairs,
A few times only, at the beginning
Of her soft-foot malady,

I should find, for a reprimand
To my gaiety, a few long grey hairs
On the breast of my coat; and one by one
I watched them float up the dark chimney.

TONY HARRISON 1937–

from LONG DISTANCE

Though my mother was already two years dead
Dad kept her slippers warming by the gas,
put hot water bottles her side of the bed
and still went to renew her transport pass.

You couldn't just drop in. You had to phone.
He'd put you off an hour to give him time
to clear away her things and look alone
as though his still raw love were such a crime.

He couldn't risk my blight of disbelief
though sure that very soon he'd hear her key
scrape in the rusted lock and end his grief.
He *knew* she'd just popped out to get the tea.

I believe life ends with death, and that is all.
You haven't both gone shopping; just the same,
in my new black leather phone book there's your name
and the disconnected number I still call.

ELAINE FEINSTEIN 1930–

DAD

Your old hat hurts me, and those black
   fat raisins you liked to press into
my palm from your soft heavy hand:
   I see you staggering back up the path
with sacks of potatoes from some local farm,
   fresh eggs, flowers. Every day I grieve

for your great heart broken and you gone.
   You loved to watch the trees. This year
you did not see their Spring.
   The sky was freezing over the fen
as on that somewhere secretly appointed day
   you beached: cold, white-faced, shivering.

What happened, old bull, my loyal
   hoarse-voiced warrior? The hammer
blow that stopped you in your track
   and brought you to a hospital monitor
could not destroy your courage
   to the end you were
uncowed and unconcerned with pleasing anyone.

I think of you now as once again safely
   at my mother's side, the earth as
chosen as a bed, and feel most sorrow for
   all that was gentle in
my childhood buried there
   already forfeit, now forever lost.

THOMAS HARDY 1840–1928

THE WALK

You did not walk with me
Of late to the hill-top tree
    By the gated ways,
    As in earlier days;
    You were weak and lame,
    So you never came,
And I went alone, and I did not mind,
Not thinking of you as left behind.

I walked up there to-day
Just in the former way:
    Surveyed around
    The familiar ground
    By myself again:
    What difference, then?
Only that underlying sense
Of the look of a room on returning thence.

LEE HARWOOD 1939–

AFRICAN VIOLETS

(for Pansy Harwood, my grandmother, 1896–1989)

Flags stream from the tops of the silver pyramids
Purple flowers present themselves to the air, the world
Chopin fights his way through all the notes, the choices

All this, and yet that emptiness

A real heart-breaker, tears in my eyes

What did I give you? At the last a pot of flowers,
your favourite colour, you said
then died soon after, the day after
I'd left you there in the bare hospital room
your eyes and voice so clear in the recognition
like so many years before   'O Travers'

And you gave me? everything I know.

But to reduce this to yet another poem
to entertain

pages of words creating old routines

I systematically smash all those pretty pictures,
they won't do anymore.
'That was a bit unnecessary, son,' you say.
I know, but their weight does you no service.

My blood is your blood,
it's as ancient as that;
pride and style that you had,
and with all a lovely generosity
I treasure.

43

I find myself moving as you would,
not the same but similar,
sharing your tastes and paths;
the night jasmine bower.

The strength of these memories
The comfort your home was

Yet it seems almost another world –
building rabbit hutches on winter evenings
in your living room, sawdust and
wood shavings on the worn carpet, easily cleared.
A house that was lived in, not exhibited.

And all those other evenings, summer or winter,
spent pickling onions, or bottling fruit,
or wrapping boxes of apples for store,
or stringing onions to hang in the shed
above the sacked potatoes,
or mending our own shoes,
all the work, cooking, making,
fixing, all done capably, easily
together.

But you now gone forever

Not sat in the corner of the couch
after your morning bath, with a cup of tea
reading the morning paper.
That ritual finished

though other 'stuff' continues
as your blood continues to flow in me
no matter what I might say
(the tense continually shifts, past and present blur)
we both love(d) love and were, are natural liars,
easy with the 'truth', turning facts to meet the story;
we both have a distaste for 'trade' –
all the contradictions happily ignored;
we both ...

Now wandering helpless around my room
the rich world about,
the flags and skies, the dreams

I talk to you again and again,
I see you again and again   sat there

EDNA EGLINTON

ATTEMPTS AT THE RATIONAL APPROACH

It isn't in important situations
that I miss you.
There is always someone who will help
when the toilet floods
or the tiles blow down.
I've learnt to wire a plug,
put up a shelf, to improvise,
make do, or go without.

I have grown a hardened shell
to wear when walking on my own
into restaurants, theatres,
cinemas and bars.

I have grown accustomed
to causing an odd number,
being partnerless at parties,
disturbing symmetry.

Till suddenly I hear the name
of a place we used to visit –
see a snippet in the paper
about an old-time friend –
think up a silly pun
which you would understand ...

I have learnt new thoughts,
new skills, tested new ventures,
found diversion in a dozen
first-time ways ...

But when the car-keys disappear
from where I left them,
when next-door's prowling cat
finds an open window,
when the sugarbowl slides off
the kitchen table –
there is no one here to shout at
but myself.

'Most near, most dear,
most loved and most far ...'

from 'To My Mother'

D.H. LAWRENCE 1885–1930

PIANO

Softly, in the dusk, a woman is singing to me;
Taking me back down the vista of years, till I see
A child sitting under the piano, in the boom of the tingling strings
And pressing the small, poised feet of a mother who smiles as she sings.

In spite of myself, the insidious mastery of song
Betrays me back, till the heart of me weeps to belong
To the old Sunday evenings at home, with winter outside
And hymns in the cosy parlour, the tinkling piano our guide.

So now it is vain for the singer to burst into clamour
With the great black piano appassionato. The glamour
Of childish days is upon me, my manhood is cast
Down in the flood of remembrance, I weep like a child for the past.

SEAMUS HEANEY 1939–

from CLEARANCES III

When all the others were away at Mass
I was all hers as we peeled potatoes.
They broke the silence, let fall one by one
Like solder weeping off the soldering iron:
Cold comforts set between us, things to share
Gleaming in a bucket of clean water.
And again let fall. Little pleasant splashes
From each other's work would bring us to our senses.

So while the parish priest at her bedside
Went hammer and tongs at the prayers for the dying
And some were responding and some crying
I remembered her head bent towards my head,
Her breath in mine, our fluent dipping knives –
Never closer the whole rest of our lives.

GEORGE BARKER 1913–91

TO MY MOTHER

Most near, most dear, most loved and most far,
Under the window where I often found her
Sitting as huge as Asia, seismic with laughter,
Gin and chicken helpless in her Irish hand,
Irresistible as Rabelais, but most tender for
The lame dogs and hurt birds that surround her, –
She is a procession no one can follow after
But be like a little dog following a brass band.

She will not glance up at the bomber, or condescend
To drop her gin and scuttle to a cellar,
But lean on the mahogany table like a mountain
Whom only faith can move, and so I send
O all my faith and all my love to tell her
That she will move from mourning into mourning.

DOUGLAS DUNN 1942–

'THIRTEEN STEPS AND THE THIRTEENTH OF MARCH'

She sat up on her pillows, receiving guests.
I brought them tea or sherry like a butler,
Up and down the thirteen steps from my pantry.
I was running out of vases.

More than one visitor came down, and said,
"Her room's so cheerful. She isn't afraid."
Even the cyclamen and lilies were listening,
Their trusty tributes holding off the real.

Doorbells, shopping, laundry, post and callers,
And twenty-six steps up the stairs
From door to bed, two times thirteen's
Unlucky numeral in my high house.

And visitors, three, four, five times a day;
My wept exhaustions over plates and cups
Drained my self-pity in these days of grief
Before the grief. Flowers, and no vases left.

Tea, sherry, biscuits, cake, and whisky for the weak . . .
She fought death with an understated mischief—
"I suppose I'll have to make an effort"—
Turning down painkillers for lucidity.

Some sat downstairs with a hankie
Nursing a little cry before going up to her.
They came back with their fears of dying amended.
"Her room's so cheerful. She isn't afraid."

Each day was duty round the clock.
Our kissing conversations kept me going,
Those times together with the phone switched off,
Remembering our lives by candlelight.

John and Stuart brought their pictures round,
A travelling exhibition. Dying,
She thumbed down some, nodded at others,
An artist and curator to the last,

Honesty at all costs. She drew up lists,
Bequests, gave things away. It tore my heart out.
Her friends assisted at this tidying
In a conspiracy of women.

At night, I lay beside her in the unique hours.
There were mysteries in candle-shadows,
Birds, aeroplanes, the rabbits of our fingers,
The lovely, erotic flame of the candlelight.

Sad? Yes. But it was beautiful also.
There was a stillness in the world. Time was out
Walking his dog by the low walls and privet.
There was anonymity in words and music.

She wanted me to wear her wedding ring.
It wouldn't fit even my little finger.
It jammed on the knuckle. I knew why.
Her fingers dwindled and her rings slipped off.

After the funeral, I had them to tea and sherry
At the Newland Park. They said it was thoughtful.
I thought it was ironic—one last time—
A mad reprisal for their loyalty.

GEORGE MACBETH 1932–92

THE SON

Her body was all stones. She lay
In the stones like a glass marble. There was
    No moisture in her. There
Was only the dry spleen and the liver
    Gone hard as pumice-stone. I closed

Her eyes. I saw a sole once on
A block of green marble. It was flung straight
    From the living brine, its
Pupils were bright with a strange heat. I watched
    A cat eat it alive. When I

Touched her cheek, the light failed. When I
Moved my open hand on her lips, there was
    No life there. She smelled of
The cheap soap we had washed her in. I saw
    The black hollows below her eyes

Where desire swam. I called her name
In the dark, but no one answered. There was
    Only the sap rising.
I thought of the clotted mercury in
    The broken thermometer of

Her body. It rose again in
My head to a silver column, a sword
    Of blood in the sun. I
Held to its cross of fire in a dream of
    Climbing. I swam in the air: my

Wings were extended into the
Night. I was borne above the clouds: I flew
    At increasing speeds, to
Increasing altitudes. There was only
    The sun above me. I *was* the

Sun. The world was my mother, I
Spread my wings to protect her growth. She broke
    Into wheat and apples
Beneath my rain. I came with my fire to
    The sea, to the earth from the air,

    To the broken ground with my fresh
Seed. I lay on her cold breast, inhaling
    The scent of iris and
Daffodils. There was nothing more to be
    Settled. I thought of her dying

    Words, how butter would scarcely melt
In her mouth. I heard a wheel squeak and the
    Drip of water. I touched
The cold rail and the covering sheet. Your
    Light shone in my eyes. Forgive me.

KEN SMITH 1938–

'YEARS GO BY' from POEM WITHOUT A TITLE

Father I say. Dad? You again?
I take your arm, your elbow,
I turn you around in the dark and I say

go back now, you're sleep walking again,
you're talking out loud again, talking in tongues
and your dream is disturbing my dream.

And none of this is any of your apples,
and even now as the centuries begin to happen
I can say: go away, you and all your violence.

Shush, now, old man.
Time to go back to your seat in the one-and-nines,
to your black bench on the Esplanade,

your name and your dates on a metal plate, back
to your own deckchair on the pier, your very own
kitchen chair tipped back on the red kitchen tiles

and you asleep, your feet up on the brass fender
and the fire banked, your cheek cocked
to the radio set, this is the 9 o'clock news Dad.

It's time. It's long past it.
Time to go back up the long pale corridor
there's no coming back from.

BRENDAN KENNELLY 1936–

I SEE YOU DANCING, FATHER

No sooner downstairs after the night's rest
And in the door
Than you started to dance a step
In the middle of the kitchen floor.

And as you danced
You whistled.
You made your own music
Always in tune with yourself.

Well, nearly always, anyway.
You're buried now
In Lislaughtin Abbey
And whenever I think of you

I go back beyond the old man
Mind and body broken
To find the unbroken man.
It is the moment before the dance begins,

Your lips are enjoying themselves
Whistling an air.
Whatever happens or cannot happen
In the time I have to spare
I see you dancing, father.

E.E. CUMMINGS 1894–1962

'MY FATHER MOVED THROUGH DOOMS OF LOVE'

my father moved through dooms of love
through sames of am through haves of give,
singing each morning out of each night
my father moved through depths of height

this motionless forgetful where
turned at his glance to shining here;
that if(so timid air is firm)
under his eyes would stir and squirm

newly as from unburied which
floats the first who,his april touch
drove sleeping selves to swarm their fates
woke dreamers to their ghostly roots

and should some why completely weep
my father's fingers brought her sleep:
vainly no smallest voice might cry
for he could feel the mountains grow.

Lifting the valleys of the sea
my father moved through griefs of joy;
praising a forehead called the moon
singing desire into begin

joy was his song and joy so pure
a heart of star by him could steer
and pure so now and now so yes
the wrists of twilight would rejoice

keen as midsummer's keen beyond
conceiving mind of sun will stand,
so strictly(over utmost him
so hugely)stood my father's dream

his flesh was flesh his blood was blood:
no hungry man but wished him food;
no cripple wouldn't creep one mile
uphill to only see him smile.

Scorning the pomp of must and shall
my father moved through dooms of feel;
his anger was as right as rain
his pity was as green as grain

septembering arms of year extend
less humbly wealth to foe and friend
than he to foolish and to wise
offered immeasurable is

proudly and(by octobering flame
beckoned)as earth will downward climb,
so naked for immortal work
his shoulders marched against the dark

his sorrow was as true as bread:
no liar looked him in the head;
if every friend became his foe
he'd laugh and build a world with snow.

My father moved through theys of we,
singing each new leaf out of each tree
(and every child was sure that spring
danced when she heard my father sing)

then let men kill which cannot share,
let blood and flesh be mud and mire,
scheming imagine,passion willed,
freedom a drug that's bought and sold

giving to steal and cruel kind,
a heart to fear,to doubt a mind,
to differ a disease of same,
conform the pinnacle of am

though dull were all we taste as bright,
bitter all utterly things sweet,
maggoty minus and dumb death
all we inherit,all bequeath

and nothing quite so least as truth
— i say though hate were why men breathe —
because my father lived his soul
love is the whole and more than all

CHARLES CAUSLEY 1917–

EDEN ROCK

They are waiting for me somewhere beyond Eden Rock:
My father, twenty-five, in the same suit
Of Genuine Irish Tweed, his terrier Jack
Still two years old and trembling at his feet.

My mother, twenty-three, in a sprigged dress
Drawn at the waist, ribbon in her straw hat,
Has spread the stiff white cloth over the grass.
Her hair, the colour of wheat, takes on the light.

She pours tea from a Thermos, the milk straight
From an old H.P. sauce bottle, a screw
Of paper for a cork; slowly sets out
The same three plates, the tin cups painted blue.

The sky whitens as if lit by three suns.
My mother shades her eyes and looks my way
Over the drifted stream. My father spins
A stone along the water. Leisurely,

They beckon to me from the other bank.
I hear them call, 'See where the stream-path is!
Crossing is not as hard as you might think.'

I had not thought that it would be like this.

HART CRANE 1899–1932

MY GRANDMOTHER'S LOVE LETTERS

There are no stars to-night
But those of memory.
Yet how much room for memory there is
In the loose girdle of soft rain.

There is even room enough
For the letters of my mother's mother,
Elizabeth,
That have been pressed so long
Into a corner of the roof
That they are brown and soft,
And liable to melt as snow.

Over the greatness of such space
Steps must be gentle.
It is all hung by an invisible white hair.
It trembles as birch limbs webbing the air.

And I ask myself:

"Are your fingers long enough to play
Old keys that are but echoes:
Is the silence strong enough
To carry back the music to its source
And back to you again
As though to her?"
Yet I would lead my grandmother by the hand
Through much of what she would not understand;
And so I stumble. And the rain continues on the roof
With such a sound of gently pitying laughter.

DYLAN THOMAS 1914–53

AFTER THE FUNERAL

(In Memory of Ann Jones)

After the funeral, mule praises, brays,
Windshake of sailshaped ears, muffle-toed tap
Tap happily of one peg in the thick
Grave's foot, blinds down the lids, the teeth in black,
The spittled eyes, the salt ponds in the sleeves,
Morning smack of the spade that wakes up sleep,
Shakes a desolate boy who slits his throat
In the dark of the coffin and sheds dry leaves,
That breaks one bone to light with a judgment clout,
After the feast of tear-stuffed time and thistles
In a room with a stuffed fox and a stale fern,
I stand, for this memorial's sake, alone
In the snivelling hours with dead, humped Ann
Whose hooded, fountain heart once fell in puddles
Round the parched worlds of Wales and drowned each sun
(Though this for her is a monstrous image blindly
Magnified out of praise; her death was a still drop;
She would not have me sinking in the holy
Flood of her heart's fame; she would lie dumb and deep
And need no druid of her broken body).
But I, Ann's bard on a raised hearth, call all
The seas to service that her wood-tongued virtue
Babble like a bellbuoy over the hymning heads,
Bow down the walls of the ferned and foxy woods
That her love sing and swing through a brown chapel,
Bless her bent spirit with four, crossing birds.
Her flesh was meek as milk, but this skyward statue
With the wild breast and blessed and giant skull
Is carved from her in a room with a wet window
In a fiercely mourning house in a crooked year.
I know her scrubbed and sour humble hands
Lie with religion in their cramp, her threadbare

Whisper in a damp word, her wits drilled hollow,
Her fist of a face died clenched on a round pain;
And sculptured Ann is seventy years of stone.
These cloud-sopped, marble hands, this monumental
Argument of the hewn voice, gesture and psalm,
Storm me forever over her grave until
The stuffed lung of the fox twitch and cry Love
And the strutting fern lay seeds on the black sill.

GERARD MANLEY HOPKINS 1844–89

TO R.B.

The fine delight that fathers thought; the strong
Spur, live and lancing like the blowpipe flame,
Breathes once and, quenchèd faster than it came,
Leaves yet the mind a mother of immortal song.
Nine months she then, nay years, nine years she long
Within her wears, bears, cares and combs the same:
The widow of an insight lost she lives, with aim
Now known and hand at work now never wrong.
    Sweet fire the sire of muse, my soul needs this;
I want the one rapture of an inspiration.
O then if in my lagging lines you miss
The roll, the rise, the carol, the creation,
My winter world, that scarcely breathes that bliss
Now, yields you, with some sighs, our explanation.

*'The greatest griefs shall find
themselves inside the smallest cage'*

from 'On the Death of a Child'

MAURA DOOLEY 1957–

GONE

You were only a bag of soft stuff
but I imagined you like a nut,
your brain beginning to pack itself
around the kernel that was me.
My limpet, my leech,
my little sucker-in of blood.
Gone. Sometimes I think we know
of nothing else, lost loves, lost lives,
the hopeless benediction of rain.

ROBERT HERRICK 1591–1674

UPON A CHILD THAT DIED

Here she lies, a pretty bud,
Lately made of flesh and blood,
Who as soon fell fast asleep
As her little eyes did peep.
Give her strewings, but not stir
The earth that lightly covers her.

ELIZABETH JENNINGS 1926–2001

CHILD BORN DEAD

What ceremony can we fit
You into now? If you had come
Out of a warm and noisy room
To this, there'd be an opposite
For us to know you by. We could
Imagine you in lively mood.

And then look at the other side,
The mood drawn out of you, the breath
Defeated by the power of death.
But we have never seen you stride
Ambitiously the world we know.
You could not come and yet you go.

But there is nothing now to mar
Your clear refusal of our world.
Not in our memories can we mould
You or distort your character.
Then all our consolation is
That grief can be as pure as this.

KATHERINE PHILIPS 1632–64

EPITAPH

On her Son H. P. at St. Syth's
Church where her body also lies Interred.

What on Earth deserves our trust?
Youth and beauty both are dust.
Long we gathering are with pain,
What one moment calls again.
Seven years childless marriage past,
A son, a son is born at last;
So exactly limbed and fair,
Full of good spirits, mien, and air,
As a long life promised,
Yet, in less than six weeks dead.
Too promising, too great a mind
In so small room to be confined:
Therefore, fit in Heaven to dwell,
He quickly broke the prison shell.
So the subtle alchimist,
Can't with Hermes' seal resist
The powerful spirit's subtler flight,
But t'will bid him long good night.
So the Sun if it arise
Half so glorious as his eyes,
Like this infant, takes a shroud,
Buried in a morning cloud.

D.J. ENRIGHT 1920–

ON THE DEATH OF A CHILD

The greatest griefs shall find themselves
    inside the smallest cage.
It's only then that we can hope to tame
    their rage,

The monsters we must live with. For
    it will not do
To hiss humanity because one human threw
Us out of heart and home. Or part

At odds with life because one baby failed
    to live.
Indeed, as little as its subject, is
    the wreath we give –

The big words fail to fit. Like giant boxes
Round small bodies. Taking up improper room,
Where so much withering is, and so much bloom.

MICHAEL ROSEN 1946–

'ONE OF US FELL OFF THE BOAT'

One of us fell off the boat. Look in our
faces, read our eyes as we come ashore.
One of us fell off the boat. We're back.
In our homes, you can see that there are
times when we hate surviving. There
are times when we think how easy to
have been him. One wave and gone.

SEAMUS HEANEY 1939–

THE SUMMER OF LOST RACHEL

Potato crops are flowering,
  Hard green plums appear
On damson trees at your back door
  And every berried briar

Is glittering and dripping
  Whenever showers plout down
On flooded hay and flooding drills.
  There's a ring around the moon.

The whole summer was waterlogged
  Yet everyone is loath
To trust the rain's soft-soaping ways
  And sentiments of growth

Because all confidence in summer's
  Unstinting largesse
Broke down last May when we laid you out
  In white, your whited face

Gashed from the accident, but still,
  So absolutely still,
And the setting sun set merciless
  And every merciful

Register inside us yearned
  To run the film back,
For you to step into the road
  Wheeling your bright-rimmed bike,

Safe and sound as usual,
  Across, then down the lane,
The twisted spokes all straightened out,
  The awful skid-marks gone.

But no. So let the downpours flood
   Our memory's riverbed
Until, in thick-webbed currents,
   The life you might have led

Wavers and tugs dreamily
   As soft-plumed waterweed
Which tempts our gaze and quietens it
   And recollects our need.

BEN JONSON 1572–1637

ON MY FIRST SON

Farewell, thou child of my right hand, and joy;
My sin was too much hope of thee, loved boy:
Seven years thou'wert lent to me, and I thee pay,
Exacted by thy fate, on the just day.
O could I lose all father now! for why
Will man lament the state he should envy,
To have so soon 'scaped world's and flesh's rage,
And, if no other misery, yet age?
Rest in soft peace, and asked, say, "Here doth lie
Ben Jonson his best piece of poetry."
For whose sake henceforth all his vows be such
As what he loves may never like too much.

DYLAN THOMAS 1914–53

A REFUSAL TO MOURN THE DEATH, BY FIRE, OF A CHILD IN LONDON

Never until the mankind making
Bird beast and flower
Fathering and all humbling darkness
Tells with silence the last light breaking
And the still hour
Is come of the sea tumbling in harness

And I must enter again the round
Zion of the water bead
And the synagogue of the ear of corn
Shall I let pray the shadow of a sound
Or sow my salt seed
In the least valley of sackcloth to mourn

The majesty and burning of the child's death.
I shall not murder
The mankind of her going with a grave truth
Nor blaspheme down the stations of the breath
With any further
Elegy of innocence and youth.

Deep with the first dead lies London's daughter,
Robed in the long friends,
The grains beyond age, the dark veins of her mother,
Secret by the unmourning water
Of the riding Thames.
After the first death, there is no other.

EDWIN MUIR 1887–1959

THE CHILD DYING

Unfriendly friendly universe,
I pack your stars into my purse,
And bid you, bid you so farewell.
That I can leave you, quite go out,
Go out, go out beyond all doubt,
My father says, is the miracle.

You are so great, and I so small:
I am nothing, you are all:
Being nothing, I can take this way.
Oh I need neither rise nor fall,
For when I do not move at all
I shall be out of all your day.

It's said some memory will remain
In the other place, grass in the rain,
Light on the land, sun on the sea,
A flitting grace, a phantom face,
But the world is out. There is no place
Where it and its ghost can ever be.

Father, father, I dread this air
Blown from the far side of despair,
The cold cold corner. What house, what hold,
What hand is there? I look and see
Nothing-filled eternity,
And the great round world grows weak and old.

Hold my hand, oh hold it fast—
I am changing! —until at last
My hand in yours no more will change,
Though yours change on. You here, I there,
So hand in hand, twin-leafed despair—
I did not know death was so strange.

'But if the while I think on thee, dear friend'

from 'Sonnet 30'

WILLIAM SHAKESPEARE 1564–1616

SONNET 30

When to the sessions of sweet silent thought
I summon up remembrance of things past,
I sigh the lack of many a thing I sought,
And with old woes new wail my dear time's waste:
Then can I drown an eye, unused to flow,
For precious friends hid in death's dateless night,
And weep afresh love's long since canceled woe,
And moan the expense of many a vanished sight:
Then can I grieve at grievances foregone,
And heavily from woe to woe tell o'er
The sad account of fore-bemoanèd moan,
Which I new pay as if not paid before.
   But if the while I think on thee, dear friend,
   All losses are restored, and sorrows end.

WILLIAM WORDSWORTH 1770–1850

from LINES WRITTEN A FEW MILES ABOVE TINTERN ABBEY, ON REVISITING THE BANKS OF THE WYE DURING A TOUR, JULY 13, 1798

Nor, perchance,
If I were not thus taught, should I the more
Suffer my genial spirits to decay:
For thou art with me, here, upon the banks
Of this fair river; thou, my dearest Friend,
My dear, dear Friend, and in thy voice I catch
The language of my former heart, and read
My former pleasures in the shooting lights
Of thy wild eyes. Oh! yet a little while
May I behold in thee what I was once,
My dear, dear Sister! And this prayer I make,
Knowing that Nature never did betray
The heart that loved her; 'tis her privilege,
Through all the years of this our life, to lead
From joy to joy: for she can so inform
The mind that is within us, so impress
With quietness and beauty, and so feed
With lofty thoughts, that neither evil tongues,
Rash judgments, nor the sneers of selfish men,
Nor greetings where no kindness is, nor all
The dreary intercourse of daily life,
Shall e'er prevail against us, or disturb
Our cheerful faith that all which we behold
Is full of blessings. Therefore let the moon
Shine on thee in thy solitary walk;
And let the misty mountain winds be free
To blow against thee: and in after years,
When these wild ecstasies shall be matured
Into a sober pleasure, when thy mind
Shall be a mansion for all lovely forms,
Thy memory be as a dwelling-place

For all sweet sounds and harmonies; Oh! then,
If solitude, or fear, or pain, or grief,
  Should be thy portion, with what healing thoughts
Of tender joy wilt thou remember me,
And these my exhortations! Nor, perchance,
If I should be, where I no more can hear
Thy voice, nor catch from thy wild eyes these gleams
Of past existence, wilt thou then forget
That on the banks of this delightful stream
We stood together; and that I, so long
A worshipper of Nature, hither came,
Unwearied in that service: rather say
With warmer love, oh! with far deeper zeal
Of holier love. Nor wilt thou then forget,
That after many wanderings, many years
Of absence, these steep woods and lofty cliffs,
And this green pastoral landscape, were to me
More dear, both for themselves, and for thy sake.

JOHN MILTON 1608–74

from LYCIDAS

Weep no more, woeful shepherds, weep no more,
For Lycidas your sorrow is not dead,
Sunk though he be beneath the watery floor,
So sinks the day-star in the ocean bed,
And yet anon repairs his drooping head,
And tricks his beams, and with new-spangled ore,
Flames in the forehead of the morning sky:
So Lycidas sunk low, but mounted high,
Through the dear might of him that walked the waves,
Where other groves, and other streams along,
With nectar pure his oozy locks he laves,
And hears the unexpressive nuptial song,
In the blest kingdoms meek of joy and love.
There entertain him all the saints above,
In solemn troops and sweet societies
That sing, and singing in their glory move,
And wipe the tears forever from his eyes.
Now, Lycidas, the shepherds weep no more;
Henceforth thou art the genius of the shore,
In thy large recompense, and shalt be good
To all that wander in that perilous flood.
    Thus sang the uncouth swain to th' oaks and rills,
While the still morn went out with sandals gray;
He touched the tender stops of various quills,
With eager thought warbling his Doric lay:
And now the sun had stretched out all the hills,
And now was dropped into the western bay;
At last he rose, and twitched his mantle blue:
Tomorrow to fresh woods, and pastures new.

CHARLES LAMB 1775–1834

THE OLD FAMILIAR FACES

I have had playmates, I have had companions
In my days of childhood, in my joyful schooldays;
All, all are gone, the old familiar faces.

I have been laughing, I have been carousing,
Drinking late, sitting late, with my bosom cronies;
All, all are gone, the old familiar faces.

I loved a love once, fairest among women:
Closed are her doors on me, I must not see her—
All, all are gone, the old familiar faces.

I have a friend, a kinder friend has no man:
Like an ingrate, I left my friend abruptly;
Left him, to muse on the old familiar faces.

Ghost-like I paced round the haunts of my childhood,
Earth seem'd a desert I was bound to traverse,
Seeking to find the old familiar faces.

Friend of my bosom, thou more than a brother,
Why wert not thou born in my father's dwelling?
So might we talk of the old familiar faces.

How some they have died, and some they have left me,
And some are taken from me; all are departed;
All, all are gone, the old familiar faces.

WILLIAM WORDSWORTH 1770–1850

'SONG' from LYRICAL BALLADS

She dwelt among th' untrodden ways
    Beside the springs of Dove,
A Maid whom there were none to praise
    And very few to love.

A Violet by a mossy stone
    Half-hidden from the Eye!
– Fair, as a star when only one
    Is shining in the sky!

She *lived* unknown, and few could know
    When Lucy ceased to be;
But she is in her Grave, and Oh!
    The difference to me.

A.E. HOUSMAN 1859–1936

TO AN ATHLETE DYING YOUNG

The time you won your town the race
We chaired you through the market-place;
Man and boy stood cheering by,
And home we brought you shoulder-high.

Today, the road all runners come,
Shoulder-high we bring you home,
And set you at your threshold down,
Townsman of a stiller town.

Smart lad, to slip betimes away
From fields where glory does not stay
And early though the laurel grows
It withers quicker than the rose.

Eyes the shady night has shut
Cannot see the record cut,
And silence sounds no worse than cheers
After earth has stopped the ears:

Now you will not swell the rout
Of lads that wore their honours out,
Runners whom renown outran
And the name died before the man.

So set, before its echoes fade,
The fleet foot on the sill of shade,
And hold to the low lintel up
The still-defended challenge-cup.

And round that early-laurelled head
Will flock to gaze the strengthless dead,
And find unwithered on its curls
The garland briefer than a girl's.

THEODORE ROETHKE 1908–63

ELEGY FOR JANE

(*My Student, Thrown by a Horse*)

I remember the neckcurls, limp and damp as tendrils;
And her quick look, a sidelong pickerel smile;
And how, once startled into talk, the light syllables leaped for her,
And she balanced in the delight of her thought,
A wren, happy, tail into the wind,
Her song trembling the twigs and small branches.
The shade sang with her;
The leaves, their whispers turned to kissing;
And the mold sang in the bleached valleys under the rose.

Oh, when she was sad, she cast herself down into such a pure depth,
Even a father could not find her:
Scraping her cheek against straw;
Stirring the clearest water.
My sparrow, you are not here,
Waiting like a fern, making a spiny shadow.
The sides of wet stones cannot console me,
Nor the moss, wound with the last light.

If only I could nudge you from this sleep,
My maimed darling, my skittery pigeon.
Over this damp grave I speak the words of my love:
I, with no rights in this matter,
Neither father nor lover.

HENRY VAUGHAN 1622–95

'THEY ARE ALL GONE
INTO THE WORLD OF LIGHT!'

They are all gone into the world of light!
    And I alone sit lingering here;
Their very memory is fair and bright,
    And my sad thoughts doth clear.

It glows and glitters in my cloudy breast
    Like stars upon some gloomy grove,
Or those faint beams in which this hill is dressed
    After the sun's remove.

I see them walking in an air of glory,
    Whose light doth trample on my days;
My days, which are at best but dull and hoary,
    Mere glimmering and decays.

O holy hope! and high humility,
    High as the heavens above!
These are your walks, and you have showed them me
    To kindle my cold love.

Dear, beauteous death! the jewel of the just,
    Shining nowhere but in the dark;
What mysteries do lie beyond thy dust,
    Could man outlook that mark!

He that hath found some fledged bird's nest may know
    At first sight if the bird be flown;
But what fair well or grove he sings in now,
    That is to him unknown.

And yet, as angels in some brighter dreams
    Call to the soul when man doth sleep,
So some strange thoughts transcend our wonted themes,
    And into glory peep.

If a star were confined into a tomb,
   Her captive flames must needs burn there;
But when the hand that locked her up gives room,
   She'll shine through all the sphere.

O Father of eternal life, and all
   Created glories under Thee!
Resume Thy spirit from this world of thrall
   Into true liberty!

Either disperse these mists, which blot and fill
   My perspective still as they pass;
Or else remove me hence unto that hill
   Where I shall need no glass.

THOM GUNN 1929–

THE MISSING

Now as I watch the progress of the plague,
The friends surrounding me fall sick, grow thin,
And drop away. Bared, is my shape less vague
– Sharply exposed and with a sculpted skin?

I do not like the statue's chill contour,
Not nowadays. The warmth investing me
Let outward through mind, limb, feeling, and more
In an involved increasing family.

Contact of friend led to another friend,
Supple entwinement through the living mass
Which for all that I knew might have no end,
Image of an unlimited embrace.

I did not just feel ease, though comfortable:
Aggressive as in some ideal of sport,
With ceaseless movement thrilling through the whole,
Their push kept me as firm as their support.

But death – Their deaths have left me less defined:
It was their pulsing presence made me clear.
I borrowed from it, I was unconfined,
Who tonight balance unsupported here,

Eyes glaring from raw marble, in a pose
Languorously part-buried in the block,
Shins perfect and no calves, as if I froze
Between potential and a finished work.

– Abandoned incomplete, shape of a shape,
In which exact detail shows the more strange,
Trapped in unwholeness, I find no escape
Back to the play of constant give and change.

PERCY BYSSHE SHELLEY 1792–1822

from ADONAIS, AN ELEGY ON
THE DEATH OF JOHN KEATS

Peace, peace! he is not dead, he doth not sleep –
He hath awakened from the dream of life –
'Tis we, who lost in stormy visions, keep
With phantoms an unprofitable strife,
And in mad trance, strike with our spirit's knife
Invulnerable nothings. – *We* decay
Like corpses in a charnel; fear and grief
Convulse us and consume us day by day,
And cold hopes swarm like worms within our living clay.

He has outsoared the shadow of our night;
Envy and calumny and hate and pain,
And that unrest which men miscall delight,
Can touch him not and torture not again;
From the contagion of the world's slow stain
He is secure, and now can never mourn
A heart grown cold, a head grown gray in vain;
Nor, when the spirit's self has ceased to burn,
With sparkless ashes load an unlamented urn.

He lives, he wakes – 'tis Death is dead, not he;
Mourn not for Adonais. – Thou young Dawn,
Turn all thy dew to splendour, for from thee
The spirit thou lamentest is not gone;
Ye caverns and ye forests, cease to moan!
Cease, ye faint flowers and fountains, and thou Air,
Which like a mourning veil thy scarf hadst thrown
O'er the abandoned Earth, now leave it bare
Even to the joyous stars which smile on its despair!

He is made one with Nature: there is heard
His voice in all her music, from the moan
Of thunder, to the song of night's sweet bird;
He is a presence to be felt and known
In darkness and in light, from herb and stone,
Spreading itself where'er that Power may move
Which has withdrawn his being to its own;
Which wields the world with never-wearied love,
Sustains it from beneath, and kindles it above.

He is a portion of the loveliness
Which once he made more lovely: he doth bear
His part, while the one Spirit's plastic stress
Sweeps through the dull dense world, compelling there,
All new successions to the forms they wear;
Torturing th' unwilling dross that checks its flight
To its own likeness, as each mass may bear;
And bursting in its beauty and its might
From trees and beasts and men into the Heaven's light.

'All my life's bliss is in the grave with thee'

from 'Remembrance'

WILLIAM SHAKESPEARE 1564–1616

'OUR REVELS NOW ARE ENDED'
from THE TEMPEST

Our revels now are ended. These our actors,
As I foretold you, were all spirits and
Are melted into air, into thin air:
And, like the baseless fabric of this vision,
The cloud-capp'd towers, the gorgeous palaces,
The solemn temples, the great globe itself,
Yea, all which it inherit, shall dissolve
And, like this insubstantial pageant faded,
Leave not a rack behind. We are such stuff
As dreams are made on, and our little life
Is rounded with a sleep.

EMILY DICKINSON 1830–86

1732

My life closed twice before its close—
It yet remains to see
If Immortality unveil
A third event to me

So huge, so hopeless to conceive
As these that twice befell.
Parting is all we know of heaven,
And all we need of hell.

ALFRED, LORD TENNYSON 1809–92

'BREAK, BREAK, BREAK'

Break, break, break,
  On thy cold gray stones, O Sea!
And I would that my tongue could utter
  The thoughts that arise in me.

O well for the fisherman's boy,
  That he shouts with his sister at play!
O well for the sailor lad,
  That he sings in his boat on the bay!

And the stately ships go on
  To their haven under the hill;
But O for the touch of a vanish'd hand,
  And the sound of a voice that is still!

Break, break, break,
  At the foot of thy crags, O Sea!
But the tender grace of a day that is dead
  Will never come back to me.

EZRA POUND 1885–1972

'AND THE DAYS ARE NOT FULL ENOUGH'

And the days are not full enough
And the nights are not full enough
And life slips by like a field mouse
       Not shaking the grass.

SIDNEY KEYES 1922–43

ELEGY

(*in memoriam S. K. K.*)

April again and it is a year again
Since you walked out and slammed the door
Leaving us tangled in your words. Your brain
Lives in the bank-book, and your eyes look up
Laughing from the carpet on the floor:
And we still drink from your silver cup.

It is a year again since they poured
the dumb ground into your mouth:
And yet we know, by some recurring word
Or look caught unawares, that you still drive
Our thoughts like the smart cobs of your youth –
When you and the world were alive.

A year again, and we have fallen on bad times
Since they gave you to the worms.
I am ashamed to take delight in these rhymes
Without grief; but you need no tears.
We shall never forget nor escape you, nor make terms
With your enemies, the swift-devouring years.

EDNA ST VINCENT MILLAY 1892–1950

'TIME DOES NOT BRING RELIEF'

Time does not bring relief; you all have lied
Who told me time would ease me of my pain!
I miss him in the weeping of the rain;
I want him at the shrinking of the tide;
The old snows melt from every mountain-side,
And last year's leaves are smoke in every lane;
But last year's bitter loving must remain
Heaped on my heart, and my old thoughts abide.
There are a hundred places where I fear
To go, – so with his memory they brim.
And entering with relief some quiet place
Where never fell his foot or shone his face
I say, 'There is no memory of him here!'
And so stand stricken, so remembering him.

EMILY JANE BRONTË 1818–48

REMEMBRANCE

Cold in the earth – and the deep snow piled above thee,
Far, far, removed, cold in the dreary grave!
Have I forgot, my only Love, to love thee,
Severed at last by Time's all-severing wave?

Now, when alone, do my thoughts no longer hover
Over the mountains, on that northern shore,
Resting their wings where heath and fern-leaves cover
Thy noble heart for ever, ever more?

Cold in the earth – and fifteen wild Decembers,
From those brown hills, have melted into spring:
Faithful, indeed, is the spirit that remembers
After such years of change and suffering!

Sweet Love of youth, forgive, if I forget thee,
While the world's tide is bearing me along;
Other desires and other hopes beset me,
Hopes which obscure, but cannot do thee wrong!

No later light has lightened up my heaven,
No second morn has ever shone for me;
All my life's bliss from thy dear life was given,
All my life's bliss is in the grave with thee.

But, when the days of golden dreams had perished,
And even Despair was powerless to destroy;
Then did I learn how existence could be cherished,
Strengthened, and fed without the aid of joy.

Then did I check the tears of useless passion –
Weaned my young soul from yearning after thine;
Sternly denied its burning wish to hasten
Down to that tomb already more than mine.

And, even yet, I dare not let it languish,
Dare not indulge in memory's rapturous pain;
Once drinking deep of that divinest anguish,
How could I seek the empty world again?

THOMAS HARDY 1840–1928

THE DARKLING THRUSH

I leant upon a coppice-gate
  When Frost was spectre-gray,
And Winter's dregs made desolate
  The weakening eye of day.
The tangled bine-stems scored the sky
  Like strings of broken lyres,
And all mankind that haunted nigh
  Had sought their household fires.

The land's sharp features seemed to be
  The Century's corpse outleant,
His crypt the cloudy canopy,
  The wind his death-lament.
The ancient pulse of germ and birth
  Was shrunken hard and dry,
And every spirit upon earth
  Seemed fervourless as I.

At once a voice arose among
  The bleak twigs overhead
In a full-hearted evensong
  Of joy illimited;
An aged thrush, frail, gaunt, and small,
  In blast-beruffled plume,
Had chosen thus to fling his soul
  Upon the growing gloom.

So little cause for carolings
    Of such ecstatic sound
Was written on terrestrial things
    Afar or nigh around,
That I could think there trembled through
    His happy good-night air
Some blessed Hope, whereof he knew
    And I was unaware.

CHIDIOCK TICHBORNE ?–1586

TICHBORNE'S ELEGY

Written with his own hand in the Tower before his execution

My prime of youth is but a frost of cares,
My feast of joy is but a dish of pain,
My crop of corn is but a field of tares,
And all my good is but vain hope of gain;
The day is past, and yet I saw no sun,
And now I live, and now my life is done.

My tale was heard and yet it was not told,
My fruit is fallen and yet my leaves are green,
My youth is spent and yet I am not old,
I saw the world and yet I was not seen;
My thread is cut and yet it is not spun,
And now I live, and now my life is done.

I sought my death and found it in my womb,
I looked for life and saw it was a shade,
I trod the earth and knew it was my tomb,
And now I die, and now I was but made;
My glass is full, and now my glass is run,
And now I live, and now my life is done.

SIR WALTER RALEGH 1552?–1618

'WHAT IS OUR LIFE?'

What is our life? a play of passion,
Our mirth the musicke of division,
Our mothers wombes the tyring houses be,
Where we are drest for this short Comedy,
Heaven the Judicious sharpe spectator is,
That sits and markes still who doth act amisse,
Our graves that hide us from the searching Sun,
Are like drawne curtaynes when the play is done,
Thus march we playing to our latest rest,
Onely we dye in earnest, that's no Jest.

ERNEST DOWSON 1867–1900

VITAE SUMMA BREVIS SPEM NOS VETAT INCOHARE LONGAM

They are not long, the weeping and the laughter,
  Love and desire and hate:
I think they have no portion in us after
  We pass the gate.

They are not long, the days of wine and roses:
  Out of a misty dream
Our path emerges for a while, then closes
  Within a dream.

PERCY BYSSHE SHELLEY 1792–1822

from ADONAIS, AN ELEGY ON THE DEATH OF JOHN KEATS

The One remains, the many change and pass;
Heaven's light forever shines, Earth's shadows fly;
Life, like a dome of many-coloured glass,
Stains the white radiance of Eternity,
Until Death tramples it to fragments. – Die,
If thou wouldst be with that which thou dost seek!
Follow where all is fled! – Rome's azure sky,
Flowers, ruins, statues, music, words, are weak
The glory they transfuse with fitting truth to speak.

Why linger, why turn back, why shrink, my Heart?
Thy hopes are gone before: from all things here
They have departed; thou shouldst now depart!
A light is past from the revolving year,
And man, and woman; and what still is dear
Attracts to crush, repels to make thee wither.
The soft sky smiles, – the low wind whispers near:
'Tis Adonais calls! oh, hasten thither,
No more let Life divide what Death can join together.

That Light whose smile kindles the Universe,
That Beauty in which all things work and move,
That Benediction which the eclipsing Curse
Of birth can quench not, that sustaining Love
Which through the web of being blindly wove
By man and beast and earth and air and sea,
Burns bright or dim, as each are mirrors of
The fire for which all thirst; now beams on me,
Consuming the last clouds of cold mortality.

The breath whose might I have invoked in song
Descends on me; my spirit's bark is driven,
Far from the shore, far from the trembling throng
Whose sails were never to the tempest given;
The massy earth and sphered skies are riven!
I am borne darkly, fearfully, afar;
Whilst burning through the inmost veil of Heaven,
The soul of Adonais, like a star,
Beacons from the abode where the Eternal are.

AMY LEVY 1861–89

EPITAPH

(On a Commonplace Person Who Died in Bed)

This is the end of him, here he lies:
The dust in his throat, the worm in his eyes,
The mould in his mouth, the turf on his breast;
This is the end of him, this is best.
He will never lie on his couch awake,
Wide-eyed, tearless, till dim daybreak.
Never again will he smile and smile
When his heart is breaking all the while.
He will never stretch out his hands in vain
Groping and groping – never again.
Never ask for bread, get a stone instead,
Never pretend that the stone is bread.
Never sway and sway 'twixt the false and true,
Weighing and noting the long hours through.
Never ache and ache with the chok'd-up sighs;
This is the end of him, here he lies.

ALUN LEWIS 1915–44

SONG

(On seeing dead bodies floating off the Cape)

The first month of his absence
I was numb and sick
And where he'd left his promise
Life did not turn or kick.
The seed, the seed of love was sick.

The second month my eyes were sunk
In the darkness of despair,
And my bed was like a grave
And his ghost was lying there.
And my heart was sick with care.

The third month of his going
I thought I heard him say
"Our course deflected slightly
On the thirty-second day – "
The tempest blew his words away.

And he was lost among the waves,
His ship rolled helpless in the sea,
The fourth month of his voyage
He shouted grievously
"Beloved, do not think of me."

The flying fish like kingfishers
Skin the sea's bewildered crests,
The whales blow steaming fountains,
The seagulls have no nests
Where my lover sways and rests.

We never thought to buy and sell
This life that blooms or withers in the leaf,
And I'll not stir, so he sleeps well,
Though cell by cell the coral reef
Builds an eternity of grief.

But oh! the drag and dullness of my Self;
The turning seasons wither in my head;
All this slowness, all this hardness,
The nearness that is waiting in my bed,
The gradual self-effacement of the dead.

W.H. AUDEN 1907–73

from TWELVE SONGS

Stop all the clocks, cut off the telephone,
Prevent the dog from barking with a juicy bone,
Silence the pianos and with muffled drum
Bring out the coffin, let the mourners come.

Let aeroplanes circle moaning overhead
Scribbling on the sky the message He Is Dead,
Put crêpe bows round the white necks of the public doves,
Let the traffic policemen wear black cotton gloves.

He was my North, my South, my East and West,
My working week and my Sunday rest,
My noon, my midnight, my talk, my song;
I thought that love would last for ever: I was wrong.

The stars are not wanted now: put out every one;
Pack up the moon and dismantle the sun;
Pour away the ocean and sweep up the wood;
For nothing now can ever come to any good.

EDNA ST VINCENT MILLAY 1892–1950

DIRGE WITHOUT MUSIC

I am not resigned to the shutting away of loving hearts in the hard ground.
So it is, and so it will be, for so it has been, time out of mind:
Into the darkness they go, the wise and the lovely. Crowned
With lilies and with laurel they go; but I am not resigned.

Lovers and thinkers, into the earth with you.
Be one with the dull, the indiscriminate dust.
A fragment of what you felt, of what you knew,
A formula, a phrase remains, – but the best is lost.

The answers quick and keen, the honest look, the laughter, the love, –
They are gone. They are gone to feed the roses. Elegant and curled
Is the blossom. Fragrant is the blossom. I know. But I do not approve.
More precious was the light in your eyes than all the roses in the world.

Down, down, down into the darkness of the grave
Gently they go, the beautiful, the tender, the kind;
Quietly they go, the intelligent, the witty, the brave.
I know. But I do not approve. And I am not resigned.

ALFRED, LORD TENNYSON 1809–92

from 'IN MEMORIAM' A. H. H.

XXVII

I envy not in any moods
   The captive void of noble rage,
   The linnet born within the cage,
That never knew the summer woods:

I envy not the beast that takes
   His license in the field of time,
   Unfetter'd by the sense of crime,
To whom a conscience never wakes;

Nor, what may count itself as blest,
   The heart that never plighted troth
   But stagnates in the weeds of sloth;
Nor any want-begotten rest.

I hold it true, whate'er befall;
   I feel it, when I sorrow most;
   'Tis better to have loved and lost
Than never to have loved at all.

'In Flanders fields the poppies blow'

from 'In Flanders Fields'

WALT WHITMAN 1819–92

'PENSIVE, ON HER DEAD GAZING,
I HEARD THE MOTHER OF ALL'

Pensive, on her dead gazing, I heard the Mother of All,
Desperate, on the torn bodies, on the forms covering the battle-fields
  gazing;
(As the last gun ceased—but the scent of the powder-smoke linger'd;)
As she call'd to her earth with mournful voice while she stalk'd:
Absorb them well, O my earth, she cried—I charge you, lose not my sons!
  lose not an atom;
And you streams, absorb them well, taking their dear blood;
And you local spots, and you airs that swim above lightly,
And all you essences of soil and growth—and you, my rivers' depths;
And you, mountain sides—and the woods where my dear children's blood,
  trickling, redden'd;
And you trees, down in your roots, to bequeath to all future trees,
My dead absorb—my young men's beautiful bodies absorb—and their
  precious, precious, precious blood;
Which holding in trust for me, faithfully back again give me many a year
  hence,
In unseen essence and odor of surface and grass, centuries hence;
In blowing airs from the fields, back again give me my darlings—give my
  immortal heroes;
Exhale me them centuries hence—breathe me their breath—let not an atom
  be lost;
O years and graves! O air and soil! O my dead, an aroma sweet!
Exhale them perennial, sweet death, years, centuries hence.

LAURENCE BINYON 1869–1943

FOR THE FALLEN (SEPTEMBER 1914)

With proud thanksgiving, a mother for her children,
England mourns for her dead across the sea.
Flesh of her flesh they were, spirit of her spirit,
Fallen in the cause of the free.

Solemn the drums thrill: Death august and royal
Sings sorrow up into immortal spheres.
There is music in the midst of desolation
And a glory that shines upon our tears.

They went with songs to the battle, they were young,
Straight of limb, true of eye, steady and aglow.
They were staunch to the end against odds uncounted,
They fell with their faces to the foe.

They shall grow not old, as we that are left grow old:
Age shall not weary them, nor the years condemn.
At the going down of the sun and in the morning
We will remember them.

They mingle not with their laughing comrades again;
They sit no more at familiar tables of home;
They have no lot in our labour of the day-time;
They sleep beyond England's foam.

But where our desires are and our hopes profound,
Felt as a well-spring that is hidden from sight,
To the innermost heart of their own land they are known
As the stars are known to the Night;

As the stars that shall be bright when we are dust,
Moving in marches upon the heavenly plain,
As the stars that are starry in the time of our darkness,
To the end, to the end, they remain.

RUPERT BROOKE 1887–1915

THE SOLDIER

If I should die, think only this of me:
   That there's some corner of a foreign field
That is for ever England. There shall be
   In that rich earth a richer dust concealed;
A dust whom England bore, shaped, made aware,
   Gave, once, her flowers to love, her ways to roam,
A body of England's, breathing English air,
   Washed by the rivers, blest by suns of home.

And think, this heart, all evil shed away,
   A pulse in the eternal mind, no less
     Gives somewhere back the thoughts by England given;
Her sights and sounds; dreams happy as her day;
   And laughter, learnt of friends; and gentleness,
     In hearts at peace, under an English heaven.

WILLIAM BUTLER YEATS 1865–1939

AN IRISH AIRMAN FORESEES HIS DEATH

I know that I shall meet my fate
Somewhere among the clouds above;
Those that I fight I do not hate,
Those that I guard I do not love;
My country is Kiltartan Cross,
My countrymen Kiltartan's poor,
No likely end could bring them loss
Or leave them happier than before.
Nor law, nor duty bade me fight,
Nor public men, nor cheering crowds,
A lonely impulse of delight
Drove to this tumult in the clouds;
I balanced all, brought all to mind,
The years to come seemed waste of breath,
A waste of breath the years behind
In balance with this life, this death.

WILFRED OWEN 1893–1918

ANTHEM FOR DOOMED YOUTH

What passing-bells for these who die as cattle?
– Only the monstrous anger of the guns.
Only the stuttering rifles' rapid rattle
Can patter out their hasty orisons.
No mockeries now for them; no prayers nor bells;
Nor any voice of mourning save the choirs, –
The shrill, demented choirs of wailing shells;
And bugles calling for them from sad shires.

What candles may be held to speed them all?
Not in the hands of boys but in their eyes
Shall shine the holy glimmers of goodbyes.
The pallor of girls' brows shall be their pall;
Their flowers the tenderness of patient minds,
And each slow dusk a drawing-down of blinds.

JOHN McCRAE 1872–1918

IN FLANDERS FIELDS

In Flanders fields the poppies blow
Between the crosses, row on row,
    That mark our place; and in the sky
    The larks, still bravely singing, fly
Scarce heard amid the guns below.

We are the Dead. Short days ago
We lived, felt dawn, saw sunset glow,
    Loved and were loved, and now we lie,
    In Flanders fields.

Take up our quarrel with the foe:
To you from failing hands we throw
    The torch; be yours to hold it high.
    If ye break faith with us who die
We shall not sleep, though poppies grow
    In Flanders fields.

IVOR GURNEY 1890–1937

TO HIS LOVE

He's gone, and all our plans
  Are useless indeed.
We'll walk no more on Cotswold
  Where the sheep feed
  Quietly and take no heed.

His body that was so quick
  Is not as you
Knew it, on Severn river
  Under the blue
  Driving our small boat through.

You would not know him now . . .
  But still he died
Nobly, so cover him over
  With violets of pride
  Purple from Severn side.

Cover him, cover him soon!
  And with thick-set
Masses of memoried flowers –
  Hide that red wet
  Thing I must somehow forget.

PHILIP LARKIN 1922–85

MCMXIV

Those long uneven lines
Standing as patiently
As if they were stretched outside
The Oval or Villa Park,
The crowns of hats, the sun
On moustached archaic faces
Grinning as if it were all
An August Bank Holiday lark;

And the shut shops, the bleached
Established names on the sunblinds,
The farthings and sovereigns,
And dark-clothed children at play
Called after kings and queens,
The tin advertisements
For cocoa and twist, and the pubs
Wide open all day;

And the countryside not caring:
The place-names all hazed over
With flowering grasses, and fields
Shadowing Domesday lines
Under wheat's restless silence;
The differently-dressed servants
With tiny rooms in huge houses,
The dust behind limousines;

Never such innocence,
Never before or since,
As changed itself to past
Without a word—the men
Leaving the gardens tidy,
The thousands of marriages
Lasting a little while longer:
Never such innocence again.

LOTTE KRAMER 1923–

POST-WAR (6)

In France there was some heirloom jewellery,
Smuggled and hidden in the Nazi years,
Now found again and mostly ownerless.
It crouched inside my palm as family

Survivor. I recognised the bracelet
And the ring, Victorian brooches set in
Filigree with weeping rubies. Secret
Histories escaping in a tin

From gas and ash, divorced from neck and arm,
The warmth that cradled them in Kaiser's time
Or later in the 20s decadence.
Now, in this island's twilight, life or chance

On certain days will bring these items out
To give them air, to mourn, to celebrate.

SEAMUS HEANEY 1939–

THE STRAND AT LOUGH BEG

In memory of Colum McCartney

All round this little island, on the strand
Far down below there, where the breakers strive,
Grow the tall rushes from the oozy sand.
Dante, Purgatorio, I. 100–3

Leaving the white glow of filling stations
And a few lonely streetlamps among fields
You climbed the hills towards Newtownhamilton
Past the Fews Forest, out beneath the stars —
Along that road, a high, bare pilgrim's track
Where Sweeney fled before the bloodied heads,
Goat-beards and dogs' eyes in a demon pack
Blazing out of the ground, snapping and squealing.
What blazed ahead of you? A faked road block?
The red lamp swung, the sudden brakes and stalling
Engine, voices, heads hooded and the cold-nosed gun?
Or in your driving mirror, tailing headlights
That pulled out suddenly and flagged you down
Where you weren't known and far from what you knew:
The lowland clays and waters of Lough Beg,
Church Island's spire, its soft treeline of yew.

There you once heard guns fired behind the house
Long before rising time, when duck shooters
Haunted the marigolds and bulrushes,
But still were scared to find spent cartridges,
Acrid, brassy, genital, ejected,
On your way across the strand to fetch the cows.
For you and yours and yours and mine fought shy,
Spoke an old language of conspirators
And could not crack the whip or seize the day:

134

Big-voiced scullions, herders, feelers round
Haycocks and hindquarters, talkers in byres,
Slow arbitrators of the burial ground.

Across that strand of yours the cattle graze
Up to their bellies in an early mist
And now they turn their unbewildered gaze
To where we work our way through squeaking sedge
Drowning in dew. Like a dull blade with its edge
Honed bright, Lough Beg half shines under the haze.
I turn because the sweeping of your feet
Has stopped behind me, to find you on your knees
With blood and roadside muck in your hair and eyes,
Then kneel in front of you in brimming grass
And gather up cold handfuls of the dew
To wash you, cousin. I dab you clean with moss
Fine as the drizzle out of a low cloud.
I lift you under the arms and lay you flat.
With rushes that shoot green again, I plait
Green scapulars to wear over your shroud.

'I have come into the hour of a white healing'

from 'Into the Hour'

ELIZABETH JENNINGS 1926–2001

INTO THE HOUR

I have come into the hour of a white healing.
Grief's surgery is over and I wear
The scar of my remorse and of my feeling.

I have come into a sudden sunlit hour
When ghosts are scared to corners. I have come
Into the time when grief begins to flower

Into a new love. It had filled my room
Long before I recognized it. Now
I speak its name. Grief finds its good way home.

The apple-blossom's handsome on the bough
And Paradise spreads round. I touch its grass.
I want to celebrate but don't know how.

I need not speak though everyone I pass
Stares at me kindly. I would put my hand
Into their hands. Now I have lost my loss

In some way I may later understand.
I hear the singing of the summer grass.
And love, I find, has no considered end,

Nor is it subject to the wilderness
Which follows death. I am not traitor to
A person or a memory. I trace

Behind that love another which is running
Around, ahead. I need not ask its meaning.

EMILY DICKINSON 1830–86

341

After great pain, a formal feeling comes—
The Nerves sit ceremonious, like Tombs—
The stiff Heart questions was it He, that bore,
And Yesterday, or Centuries before?

The Feet, mechanical, go round—
Of Ground, or Air, or Ought—
A Wooden way
Regardless grown,
A Quartz contentment, like a stone—

This is the Hour of Lead—
Remembered, if outlived,
As Freezing persons, recollect the Snow—
First— Chill— then Stupor— then the letting go—

ALFRED, LORD TENNYSON 1890–92

from 'IN MEMORIAM' A. H. H.

CXXIX

Dear friend, far off, my lost desire,
    So far, so near in woe and weal;
    O loved the most, when most I feel
There is a lower and a higher;

Known and unknown; human, divine;
    Sweet human hand and lips and eye;
    Dear heavenly friend that canst not die,
Mine, mine, for ever, ever mine;

Strange friend, past, present, and to be;
    Loved deeplier, darklier understood;
    Behold, I dream a dream of good,
And mingle all the world with thee.

CXXX

Thy voice is on the rolling air;
    I hear thee where the waters run;
    Thou standest in the rising sun,
And in the setting thou art fair.

What art thou then? I cannot guess;
    But tho' I seem in star and flower
    To feel thee some diffusive power,
I do not therefore love thee less:

My love involves the love before;
    My love is vaster passion now;
    Tho' mix'd with God and Nature thou,
I seem to love thee more and more.

Far off thou art, but ever nigh;
   I have thee still, and I rejoice;
   I prosper, circled with thy voice;
I shall not lose thee tho' I die.

CXXXI
O living will that shalt endure
   When all that seems shall suffer shock,
   Rise in the spiritual rock,
Flow thro' our deeds and make them pure,

That we may lift from out of dust
   A voice as unto him that hears,
   A cry above the conquer'd years
To one that with us works, and trust,

With faith that comes of self-control,
   The truths that never can be proved
   Until we close with all we loved,
And all we flow from, soul in soul.

ELINOR WYLIE 1885–1928

FAREWELL, SWEET DUST

Now I have lost you, I must scatter
All of you on the air henceforth;
Not that to me it can ever matter
But it's only fair to the rest of earth.

Now especially, when it is winter
And the sun's not half so bright as he was,
Who wouldn't be glad to find a splinter
That once was you, in the frozen grass?

Snowflakes, too, will be softer feathered,
Clouds, perhaps, will be whiter plumed;
Rain, whose brilliance you caught and gathered,
Purer silver have reassumed.

Farewell, sweet dust; I was never a miser:
Once, for a minute, I made you mine:
Now you are gone, I am none the wiser
But the leaves of the willow are bright as wine.

THOMAS HARDY 1840–1928

AFTER A JOURNEY

Hereto I come to view a voiceless ghost;
    Whither, O whither will its whim now draw me?
Up the cliff, down, till I'm lonely, lost,
    And the unseen waters' ejaculations awe me.
Where you will next be there's no knowing,
    Facing round about me everywhere,
        With your nut-coloured hair,
And gray eyes, and rose-flush coming and going.

Yes: I have re-entered your olden haunts at last;
    Through the years, through the dead scenes I have tracked you;
What have you now found to say of our past –
    Scanned across the dark space wherein I have lacked you?
Summer gave us sweets, but autumn wrought division?
    Things were not lastly as firstly well
        With us twain, you tell?
But all's closed now, despite Time's derision.

I see what you are doing: you are leading me on
    To the spots we knew when we haunted here together,
The waterfall, above which the mist-bow shone
    At the then fair hour in the then fair weather,
And the cave just under, with a voice still so hollow
    That it seems to call out to me from forty years ago,
        When you were all aglow,
And not the thin ghost that I now frailly follow!

Ignorant of what there is flitting here to see,
    The waked birds preen and the seals flop lazily,
Soon you will have, Dear, to vanish from me,
    For the stars close their shutters and the dawn whitens hazily.
Trust me, I mind not, though Life lours,
    The bringing me here; nay, bring me here again!
        I am just the same as when
Our days were a joy, and our paths through flowers.

144

HENRY WADSWORTH LONGFELLOW 1807–82

THE CROSS OF SNOW

In the long, sleepless watches of the night,
    A gentle face – the face of one long dead –
    Looks at me from the wall, where round its head
    The night-lamp casts a halo of pale light.
Here in this room she died; and soul more white
    Never through martyrdom of fire was led
    To its repose; nor can in books be read
    The legend of a life more benedight.
There is a mountain in the distant West
    That, sun-defying, in its deep ravines
    Displays a cross of snow upon its side.
Such is the cross I wear upon my breast
    These eighteen years, through all the changing scenes
    And seasons, changeless since the day she died.

THOM GUNN 1929–

THE REASSURANCE

About ten days or so
After we saw you dead
You came back in a dream.
I'm all right now you said.

And it *was* you, although
You were fleshed out again:
You hugged us all round then,
And gave your welcoming beam.

How like you to be kind,
Seeking to reassure.
And, yes, how like my mind
To make itself secure.

CHRISTINA ROSSETTI 1830–94

SONG

When I am dead, my dearest,
   Sing no sad songs for me;
Plant thou no roses at my head,
   Nor shady cypress tree:
Be the green grass above me
   With showers and dewdrops wet;
And if thou wilt, remember,
   And if thou wilt, forget.

I shall not see the shadows,
   I shall not feel the rain;
I shall not hear the nightingale
   Sing on, as if in pain:
And dreaming through the twilight
   That doth not rise nor set,
Haply I may remember,
   And haply may forget.

DONALD DAVIE 1922–95

TIME PASSING, BELOVED

Time passing, and the memories of love
Coming back to me, carissima, no more mockingly
Than ever before; time passing, unslackening,
Unhastening, steadily; and no more
Bitterly, beloved, the memories of love
Coming into the shore.

How will it end? Time passing and our passages of love
As ever, beloved, blind
As ever before; time binding, unbinding
About us; and yet to remember
Never less chastening, nor the flame of love
Less like an ember.

What will become of us? Time
Passing, beloved, and we in a sealed
Assurance unassailed
By memory. How can it end,
This siege of a shore that no misgivings have steeled,
No doubts defend?

WILLIAM SHAKESPEARE 1564–1616

'FEAR NO MORE THE HEAT O' THE SUN'
from CYMBELINE

Fear no more the heat o' the sun,
  Nor the furious winter's rages;
Thou thy worldly task hast done,
  Home art gone, and ta'en thy wages:
Golden lads and girls all must,
As chimney-sweepers, come to dust.

Fear no more the frown o' the great;
  Thou art past the tyrant's stroke;
Care no more to clothe and eat;
  To thee the reed is as the oak:
The scepter, learning, physic, must
All follow this, and come to dust.

Fear no more the lightning flash,
  Nor the all-dreaded thunder stone;
Fear not slander, censure rash;
  Thou hast finished joy and moan:
All lovers young, all lovers must
Consign to thee, and come to dust.

No exorciser harm thee!
Nor no witchcraft charm thee!
Ghost unlaid forbear thee!
Nothing ill come near thee!
Quiet consummation have;
And renownèd be thy grave!

STEPHEN SPENDER 1909–95

'I THINK CONTINUALLY OF THOSE WHO WERE TRULY GREAT'

I think continually of those who were truly great.
Who, from the womb, remembered the soul's history
Through corridors of light where the hours are suns
Endless and singing. Whose lovely ambition
Was that their lips, still touched with fire,
Should tell of the Spirit clothed from head to foot in song.
And who hoarded from the Spring branches
The desires falling across their bodies like blossoms.

What is precious is never to forget
The essential delight of the blood drawn from ageless springs
Breaking through rocks in worlds before our earth.
Never to deny its pleasure in the morning simple light
Nor its grave evening demand for love.
Never to allow gradually the traffic to smother
With noise and fog the flowering of the spirit.

Near the snow, near the sun, in the highest fields
See how these names are fêted by the waving grass
And by the streamers of white cloud
And whispers of wind in the listening sky.
The names of those who in their lives fought for life
Who wore at their hearts the fire's centre.
Born of the sun they travelled a short while towards the sun,
And left the vivid air signed with their honour.

THOM GUNN 1929–

MY SAD CAPTAINS

One by one they appear in
the darkness: a few friends, and
a few with historical
names. How late they start to shine!
but before they fade they stand
perfectly embodied, all

the past lapping them like a
cloak of chaos. They were men
who, I thought, lived only to
renew the wasteful force they
spent with each hot convulsion.
They remind me, distant now.

True, they are not at rest yet,
but now that they are indeed
apart, winnowed from failures,
they withdraw to an orbit
and turn with disinterested
hard energy, like the stars.

CHRISTINA ROSSETTI 1830–94

REMEMBER

Remember me when I am gone away,
  Gone far away into the silent land;
  When you can no more hold me by the hand,
Nor I half turn to go yet turning stay.
Remember me when no more day by day
  You tell me of our future that you planned:
  Only remember me; you understand
It will be late to counsel then or pray.
Yet if you should forget me for a while
  And afterwards remember, do not grieve:
  For if the darkness and corruption leave
  A vestige of the thoughts that once I had,
Better by far you should forget and smile
  Than that you should remember and be sad.

WILLIAM SHAKESPEARE 1564–1616

SONNET 29

When, in disgrace with fortune and men's eyes,
I all alone beweep my outcast state,
And trouble deaf heaven with my bootless cries,
And look upon myself, and curse my fate,
Wishing me like to one more rich in hope,
Featured like him, like him with friends possessed,
Desiring this man's art and that man's scope,
With what I most enjoy contented least;
Yet in these thoughts myself almost despising,
Haply I think on thee – and then my state,
Like to the lark at break of day arising
From sullen earth, sings hymns at heaven's gate;
  For thy sweet love rememb'red such wealth brings
  That then I scorn to change my state with kings.

'In my end is my beginning'

from East Coker

SIEGFRIED SASSOON 1886–1967

EVERYONE SANG

Everyone suddenly burst out singing;
And I was filled with such delight
As prisoned birds must find in freedom,
Winging wildly across the white
Orchards and dark-green fields; on—on—and out of sight.

Everyone's voice was suddenly lifted;
And beauty came like the setting sun:
My heart was shaken with tears; and horror
Drifted away ... O, but Everyone
Was a bird; and the song was wordless; the singing will never be done.

ANON

'WEEP YOU NO MORE, SAD FOUNTAINS'

Weep you no more, sad fountains;
   What need you flow so fast?
Look how the snowy mountains
   Heaven's sun doth gently waste.
   But my sun's heavenly eyes
      View not your weeping,
      That now lie sleeping
   Softly, now softly lies
      Sleeping.

Sleep is a reconciling,
   A rest that peace begets.
Doth not the sun rise smiling
   When fair at even he sets?
   Rest you then, rest, sad eyes,
      Melt not in weeping
      While she lies sleeping
   Softly, now softly lies
      Sleeping.

JOYCE GRENFELL 1910–79

'IF I SHOULD GO BEFORE THE REST OF YOU'

If I should go before the rest of you,
Break not a flower nor inscribe a stone.
Nor when I'm gone speak in a Sunday voice,
But be the usual selves that I have known.
    Weep if you must,
    Parting is hell,
    But life goes on,
    So sing as well.

ANN THORP

BELIEF

I have to believe
That you still exist
Somewhere,
That you still watch me
Sometimes,
That you still love me
Somehow.

I have to believe
That life has meaning
Somehow,
That I am useful here
Sometimes,
That I make small differences
Somewhere.

I have to believe
That I need to stay here
For some time,
That all this teaches me
Something,
So that I can meet you again
Somewhere.

LOUISE BOGAN 1897–1970

NIGHT

The cold remote islands
And the blue estuaries
Where what breathes, breathes
The restless wind of the inlets,
And what drinks, drinks
The incoming tide;

Where shell and weed
Wait upon the salt wash of the sea,
And the clear nights of stars
Swing their lights westward
To set behind the land;

Where the pulse clinging to the rocks
Renews itself forever;
Where, again on cloudless nights,
The water reflects
The firmament's partial setting;

– O remember
In your narrowing dark hours
That more things move
Than blood in the heart.

SIR WALTER RALEGH 1552?–1618

THE PASSIONATE MAN'S PILGRIMAGE

Give me my scallop-shell of quiet,
My staff of faith to walk upon,
My scrip of joy, immortal diet,
My bottle of salvation,
My gown of glory, hope's true gage,
And thus I'll take my pilgrimage.

Blood must be my body's balmer,
No other balm will there be given,
Whilst my soul like a white palmer
Travels to the land of heaven,
Over the silver mountains,
Where spring the nectar fountains;
And there I'll kiss
The bowl of bliss,
And drink my eternal fill
On every milken hill.
My soul will be a-dry before,
But after it will ne'er thirst more;
And by the happy blissful way
More peaceful pilgrims I shall see
That have shook off their gowns of clay
And go appareled fresh like me.
I'll bring them first
To slake their thirst,
And then to taste those nectar suckets,
At the clear wells
Where sweetness dwells,
Drawn up by saints in crystal buckets.

And when our bottles and all we
Are filled with immortality,
Then the holy paths we'll travel,
Strewed with rubies thick as gravel,

Ceilings of diamonds, sapphire floors,
High walls of coral, and pearl bowers,
From thence to heaven's bribeless hall
Where no corrupted voices brawl,
No conscience molten into gold,
Nor forged accusers bought and sold,
No cause deferred, nor vain-spent journey,
For there Christ is the king's attorney,
Who pleads for all, without degrees,
And he hath angels, but no fees.
When the grand twelve million jury
Of our sins and sinful fury,
'Gainst our souls black verdicts give,
Christ pleads his death, and then we live.
Be thou my speaker, taintless pleader,
Unblotted lawyer, true proceeder;
Thou movest salvation even for alms,
Not with a bribed lawyer's palms.
And this is my eternal plea
To him that made heaven, earth, and sea,
Seeing my flesh must die so soon,
And want a head to dine next noon,
Just at the stroke when my veins start and spread,
Set on my soul an everlasting head.
Then am I ready, like a palmer fit,
To tread those blest paths which before I writ.

ARTHUR HUGH CLOUGH 1819–61

'SAY NOT THE STRUGGLE NOUGHT AVAILETH'

Say not the struggle nought availeth,
   The labor and the wounds are vain,
The enemy faints not, nor faileth,
   And as things have been, things remain.

If hopes were dupes, fears may be liars;
   It may be, in yon smoke concealed,
Your comrades chase e'en now the fliers,
   And, but for you, possess the field.

For while the tired waves, vainly breaking,
   Seem here no painful inch to gain
Far back through creeks and inlets making
   Came, silent, flooding in, the main,

And not by eastern windows only,
   When daylight comes, comes in the light,
In front the sun climbs slow, how slowly,
   But westward, look, the land is bright.

JOHN GILLESPIE MAGEE 1922–41

HIGH FLIGHT

Oh! I have slipped the surly bonds of Earth
And danced the skies on laughter-silvered wings;
Sunward I've climbed, and joined the tumbling mirth
Of sun-split clouds – and done a hundred things
You have not dreamed of – wheeled and soared and swung
High in the sunlit silence. Hov'ring there,
I've chased the shouting wind along, and flung
My eager craft through footless halls of air ...
Up, up the long, delirious burning blue
I've topped the wind-swept heights with easy grace,
Where never lark, or even eagle flew –
And, while with silent, lifting mind I've trod
The high untrespassed sanctity of space,
Put out my hand and touched the face of God.

WILLIAM SHAKESPEARE

SONNET 55

Not marble, nor the gilded monuments
Of princes, shall outlive this powerful rhyme;
But you shall shine more bright in these contènts
Than unswept stone, besmeared with sluttish time.
When wasteful war shall statues overturn,
And broils root out the work of masonry,
Nor Mars his sword nor war's quick fire shall burn
The living record of your memory.
'Gainst death and all-oblivious enmity
Shall you pace forth; your praise shall still find room
Even in the eyes of all posterity
That wear this world out to the ending doom.
    So, till the judgment that yourself arise,
    You live in this, and dwell in lovers' eyes.

ANON

'DO NOT STAND AT MY GRAVE AND WEEP'

Do not stand at my grave and weep;
I am not there. I do not sleep.
I am a thousand winds that blow.
I am the diamond glints on snow.
I am the sunlight on ripened grain.
I am the gentle autumn rain.
When you awaken in the morning's hush
I am the swift uplifting rush
Of quiet birds in circled flight.
I am the soft stars that shine at night.
Do not stand at my grave and cry;
I am not there. I did not die.

JOHN DONNE 1572–1631

SONNET 6 from HOLY SONNETS: DIVINE MEDITATIONS

Death be not proud, though some have called thee
Mighty and dreadfull, for, thou art not soe,
For, those, whom thou think'st, thou dost overthrow,
Die not, poore death, nor yet canst thou kill mee;
From rest and sleepe, which but thy pictures bee,
Much pleasure, then from thee, much more must flow,
And soonest our best men with thee doe goe,
Rest of their bones, and soules deliverie.
Thou art slave to Fate, chance, kings, and desperate men,
And dost with poyson, warre, and sicknesse dwell,
And poppie, or charmes can make us sleepe as well,
And better than thy stroake; why swell'st thou then?
One short sleepe past, wee wake eternally,
And death shall be no more, Death thou shalt die.

WILLIAM WORDSWORTH 1770–1850

from ODE (INTIMATIONS OF IMMORTALITY FROM RECOLLECTIONS OF EARLY CHILDHOOD)

O joy! that in our embers
Is something that doth live,
That nature yet remembers
What was so fugitive!
The thought of our past years in me doth breed
Perpetual benedictions: not indeed
For that which is most worthy to be blest;
Delight and liberty, the simple creed
Of Childhood, whether fluttering or at rest,
With new-born hope for ever in his breast:–
        Not for these I raise
        The song of thanks and praise;
    But for those obstinate questionings
    Of sense and outward things,
    Fallings from us, vanishings;
    Blank misgivings of a Creature
Moving about in worlds not realized,
High instincts, before which our mortal Nature
Did tremble like a guilty Thing surprized:
    But for those first affections,
    Those shadowy recollections,
        Which, be they what they may,
Are yet the fountain light of all our day,
Are yet a master light of all our seeing;
        Uphold us, cherish us, and make
Our noisy years seem moments in the being
Of the eternal Silence: truths that wake,
        To perish never;
Which neither listlessness, nor mad endeavour,
        Nor Man nor Boy,
Nor all that is at enmity with joy,
Can utterly abolish or destroy!
        Hence, in a season of calm weather,

Though inland far we be,
Our Souls have sight of that immortal sea
Which brought us hither,
Can in a moment travel thither,
And see the Children sport upon the shore,
And hear the mighty waters rolling evermore.

Then, sing ye Birds, sing, sing a joyous song!
And let the young Lambs bound
As to the tabor's sound!
We in thought will join your throng,
Ye that pipe and ye that play,
Ye that through your hearts to day
Feel the gladness of the May!
What though the radiance which was once so bright
Be now for ever taken from my sight,
Though nothing can bring back the hour
Of splendour in the grass, of glory in the flower;
We will grieve not, rather find
Strength in what remains behind,
In the primal sympathy
Which having been must ever be,
In the soothing thoughts that spring
Out of human suffering,
In the faith that looks through death,
In years that bring the philosophic mind.

And oh ye Fountains, Meadows, Hills, and Groves,
Think not of any severing of our loves!
Yet in my heart of hearts I feel your might;
I only have relinquished the delight
To live beneath your more habitual sway.
I love the Brooks which down their channels fret,
Even more than when I tripped lightly as they;
The innocent brightness of a new-born Day
            Is lovely yet;
The Clouds that gather round the setting sun
Do take a sober colouring from an eye
That hath kept watch o'er man's mortality;
  Another race hath been, and other palms are won.
  Thanks to the human heart by which we live,
  Thanks to its tenderness, its joys, and fears,
  To me the meanest flower that blows can give
  Thoughts that do often lie too deep for tears.

DYLAN THOMAS 1914–53

'AND DEATH SHALL HAVE NO DOMINION'

And death shall have no dominion.
Dead men naked they shall be one
With the man in the wind and the west moon;
When their bones are picked clean and the clean bones gone,
They shall have stars at elbow and foot;
Though they go mad they shall be sane,
Though they sink through the sea they shall rise again;
Though lovers be lost love shall not;
And death shall have no dominion.

And death shall have no dominion.
Under the windings of the sea
They lying long shall not die windily;
Twisting on racks when sinews give way,
Strapped to a wheel, yet they shall not break;
Faith in their hands shall snap in two,
And the unicorn evils run them through;
Split all ends up they shan't crack;
And death shall have no dominion.

And death shall have no dominion.
No more may gulls cry at their ears
Or waves break loud on the seashores;
Where blew a flower may a flower no more
Lift its head to the blows of the rain;
Though they be mad and dead as nails,
Heads of the characters hammer through daisies;
Break in the sun till the sun breaks down,
And death shall have no dominion.

T.S. ELIOT 1888–1965

from EAST COKER

Home is where one starts from. As we grow older
The world becomes stranger, the pattern more complicated
Of dead and living. Not the intense moment
Isolated, with no before and after,
But a lifetime burning in every moment
And not the lifetime of one man only
But of old stones that cannot be deciphered.
There is a time for the evening under starlight,
A time for the evening under lamplight
(The evening with the photograph album).
Love is most nearly itself
When here and now cease to matter.
Old men ought to be explorers
Here or there does not matter
We must be still and still moving
Into another intensity
For a further union, a deeper communion
Through the dark cold and the empty desolation,
The wave cry, the wind cry, the vast waters
Of the petrel and the porpoise. In my end is my beginning.

ANON

ECCLESIASTES 3.1–8

To everything there is a season, and a time to every purpose under the heaven:
a time to be born and a time to die; a time to plant, and a time to pluck up
that which is planted; a time to kill, and a time to heal; a time to break down,
and a time to build up; a time to weep and a time to laugh; a time to mourn,
and a time to dance; a time to cast away stones, and a time to gather stones
together; a time to embrace, and a time to refrain from embracing; a time
to seek, and a time to lose; a time to keep, and a time to cast away; a time to
rend, and a time to sew; a time to keep silence, and a time to speak; a time
to love, and a time to hate; a time for war, and a time for peace.

ACKNOWLEDGEMENTS

— ◇ —

The publishers would like to acknowledge the following for permission to reproduce copyright material. Every effort has been made to trace copyright holders but in a few cases this has proved impossible. The publishers would be interested to hear from any copyright holders not here acknowledged.

22, 132. Faber and Faber Ltd for 'An Arundel Tomb' and 'MCMXIV' from *Collected Poems* by Philip Larkin.
25. David Higham Associates for the extract from 'Autumn Journal' from *Collected Poems* by Louis MacNeice (Faber and Faber).
28. Faber and Faber Ltd for 'The Stone' from *Moortown* by Ted Hughes.
31, 126. The Society of Authors as the Literary Representative of the Estate of Laurence Binyon for 'Winter Sunrise' and 'For the Fallen (September 1914)'.
33. The Estate of W.S. Graham for 'Lines on Roger Hilton's Watch' from *Collected Poems 1942–1977*. Copyright Michael and Margaret Snow.
39, 51. Pollinger Ltd and the Estate of Frieda Lawrence Ravagli for 'Sorrow' and 'Piano' from *The Complete Poems of D.H. Lawrence*.
40. Gordon Dickerson for 'II' from 'Long Distance', from *Selected Poems* by Tony Harrison (Viking, 1987). Copyright © Tony Harrison.
41. Carcanet Press Ltd for 'Dad' from *Collected Poems* by Elaine Feinstein (2002).
43. 'African Violets' is from *Morning Light* by Lee Harwood (Slow Dancer Press, 1998). Reprinted by permission of the author.
52, 77. Faber and Faber Ltd for the extract from 'Clearances III' and 'The Summer of Lost Rachel' from *The Haw Lantern* by Seamus Heaney.
53. Faber and Faber Ltd for 'To My Mother' from *Collected Poems* by George Barker.
54. Faber and Faber Ltd for 'Thirteen Steps and the Thirteenth of March' from *Elegies* by Douglas Dunn.
56. Sheil Land Associates for 'The Son' from *Collected Poems 1958–1982* by George MacBeth, published by Hutchinson.
58. Bloodaxe Books for 'Years go by' from 'Poem Without a Title', from *Shed: Poems 1980–2001* by Ken Smith (Bloodaxe Books, 2002).
59. Bloodaxe Books for 'I See You Dancing, Father' from *A Time for Voices: Selected Poems 1960–1990* by Brendan Kennelly (Bloodaxe Books, 1990).
60. 'my father moved through dooms of love' is reprinted from *Complete Poems 1904–1962* by E.E. Cummings, edited by George J. Firmage, by permission of W.W. Norton & Company. Copyright © 1991 by the Trustees for the E.E. Cummings Trust and George James Firmage.
63. David Higham Associates for 'Eden Rock' from *Collected Poems* by Charles Causley (Macmillan).

175

64. 'My Grandmother's Love Letters', from *Complete Poems of Hart Crane* by Hart Crane, edited by Marc Simon. Copyright 1933, 1958, 1966 by Liveright Publishing Corporation. Copyright © 1986 by Marc Simon. Used by permission of Liveright Publishing Corporation.

65, 80, 172. David Higham Associates for 'After the Funeral', 'A Refusal to Mourn the Death, by Fire, of a Child in London' and 'And Death Shall Have No Dominion' from *Collected Poems* by Dylan Thomas (Dent).

71. Bloodaxe Books for 'Gone' from *Sound Barrier: Poems 1982–2002* by Maura Dooley (Bloodaxe Books, 2002).

73, 139. David Higham Associates for 'Child Born Dead' and 'Into the Hour' from *Collected Poems* by Elizabeth Jennings (Carcanet Press).

75. Watson, Little Limited for 'On the Death of a Child' from *Collected Poems* by D.J. Enright (Oxford University Press, 1998).

76. 'One of us fell off the boat ...' is from *Carrying the Elephant* by Michael Rosen (Penguin Books, 2002) copyright © Michael Rosen, 2002. Reproduced by permission of Penguin Books Ltd.

81. Faber and Faber Ltd for 'The Child Dying' from *Collected Poems* by Edwin Muir.

91. The Society of Authors as the Literary Representative of the Estate of A.E. Housman for 'To an Athlete Dying Young'.

92. Faber and Faber Ltd for 'Elegy for Jane' from *Collected Poems* by Theodore Roethke.

95, 146. Faber and Faber Ltd for 'The Missing' and 'The Reassurance' from *The Man with Night Sweats* by Thom Gunn.

102, 140. Poems 1732 ('My life closed twice before its close') and 341 ('After great pain, a formal feeling comes') are reprinted by permission of the publishers and Trustees of Amherst College from *The Poems of Emily Dickinson*, Thomas H. Johnson, ed., Cambridge, Mass.: The Belknap Press of Harvard University Press, Copyright © 1951, 1955, 1979 by the President and Fellows of Harvard College.

104. Faber and Faber Ltd for 'And the days are not full enough' from *Personae* by Ezra Pound.

105. Carcanet Press Ltd for 'Elegy' from *Collected Poems* (2002) by Sidney Keyes.

106, 120. 'Time Does Not Bring Relief' and 'Dirge Without Music' by Edna St Vincent Millay. From Collected Poems (HarperCollins). Copyright © 1917, 1928, 1945, 1955 by Edna St Vincent Millay and Norma Millay Ellis. All rights reserved. Reprinted by permission of Elizabeth Barnett, literary executor.

117. 'Song' from *Collected Poems* by Alun Lewis (Seren, 1994) is reprinted by permission of the Estate of Alun Lewis.

119. Faber and Faber Ltd for 'Twelve Songs IX' ('Funeral Blues') from *Collected Poems* by W.H. Auden.

128. A.P. Watt Ltd on behalf of Michael B. Yeats for 'An Irish Airman Foresees His Death' from *The Collected Poems of W.B. Yeats*.

131. The Ivor Gurney Trust for 'To His Love' by Ivor Gurney.

133. 'Post-War (6)' is from *Earthquake and Other Poems* by Lotte Kramer (Rockingham Press, 1994). Reprinted by permission of the author.

134. Faber and Faber Ltd for 'The Strand at Lough Beg' from *Field Work* by Seamus Heaney.

148. Carcanet Press Ltd for 'Time Passing, Beloved' from *Collected Poems* (1990) by Donald Davie.

150. Faber and Faber Ltd for 'I Think Continually of Those Who Were Truly Great' from *Collected Poems* by Stephen Spender.

151. Faber and Faber Ltd for 'My Sad Captains' from *My Sad Captains* by Thom Gunn.

157. 'Everyone Sang' by Siegfried Sassoon. Copyright Siegfried Sassoon by kind permission of George Sassoon.

159. Sheil Land Associates for 'If I Should Go Before the Rest of You' by Joyce Grenfell. Copyright © Joyce Grenfell 1980.

161. 'Night' from *The Blue Estuaries* by Louise Bogan. Copyright © 1968 by Louise Bogan. Copyright renewed by Ruth Limmer. Reprinted by permission of Farrar, Straus and Giroux, LLC.

165. 'High Flight' is reproduced from *John Magee, the Pilot Poet* published by This England Books (Cheltenham) UK.

173. Faber and Faber Ltd for the extract from 'East Coker' from *Four Quartets*, from *Collected Poems* by T.S. Eliot.

INDEX OF POETS' NAMES

— e —

178

INDEX OF FIRST LINES

— ◇ —